Beginning Of A Miracle

How to Intervene With the Addicted or Alcoholic Person

M. David (Mick) Meagher

Health Communications, Inc.
Pompano Beach, Florida

M. David Meagher
Nova Vita Incorporated
Del Mar, California

Library of Congress Cataloging-in-Publication Data
Filed

ISBN 0-932194-47-8

Published by Health Communications, Inc.
1721 Blount Road
Pompano Beach, Florida 33069

Acknowledgments

The undertaking of writing this book allowed me to relive many wonderful memories. The opportunity to realize how many exceptional people have entered my life, and more importantly, how many exceptional people have allowed me into their lives.

To recognize all who have shaped this book would by its nature be a long list. In some situations it would involve violating the confidence of the intervention that we planned together, something that cannot be done.

However, for my own needs I would like to express my profound gratitude to the following people and organizations for all they have given to me. It is my hope that those not specifically mentioned will know that their importance has not been lost to me.

The first opportunity I was given to work with recovery was given to me by the U.S. Marine Corps. As an active duty member I was trained in the Navy's Alcoholism Treatment Specialist Course, Naval Station, San Diego. Through the excellent training and working at a Navy treatment center for two years I was provided a learning experience seldom matched.

To Vernon Johnson, D.D., founder of the Johnson Institute, where I learned the skills of intervention, and that openness to what the addicted person tells us in their cry for help is seldom what it appears to be on the surface. Yet it is most surely the entrance to the bridge from suffering to surrender.

To Len Baltzer, former director at the McDonald Center for Treatment of Alcoholism and Drug Addiction, Scripps Memorial Hospital and currently at Community Hospital in Monterey, California. During my time at Scripps he encouraged my growth as a person and as a professional. Always willing to listen, he led through example. He showed the three keys of a successful intervention go way beyond intervention.

And, most importantly, to the families, professional groups and many others who trusted me as they brought me into their most painful and private moments so that together we could see the BEGINNING OF A MIRACLE.

When Should You Intervene?

Is the use of alcohol or other drugs causing problems in:

_____ Work or School
_____ With the law
_____ Family finances
_____ The health of the user
_____ Family gatherings
_____ Social settings
_____ Emotional stability

Following a drinking or other drug-using episode by the person you are concerned about have you felt:

_____ Embarrassed or afraid of what others might think
_____ Scared
_____ Upset or angry
_____ If you were a better parent/spouse/friend, it wouldn't have occurred
_____ Confused about what you can do

Have there been:

_____ Family fights (separations or threats of divorce) caused by the chemical use

_____ Promises or attempts to quit or control the chemical use

_____ Attempts by family members to control the chemical use

If you have answered yes to more than three of these questions, you will have enough information to intervene.

Contents

1

Overview of the Problem

The disease of addiction seems to be unparalleled in its ability to baffle, confound and eventually destroy all that it touches. Once promising careers, loving homes, special people, all are consumed by this complex and misunderstood problem.

If someone you care about is having problems caused by chemical use, the chances are you have sought answers. You want to know what you can do to help. You may already have received advice from well intentioned people that is biased or based on a misunderstanding of the problem being faced. To help, you need facts.

This is a practical guide for any reader interested in interrupting the destructive course of chemical dependency. It will help you recognize that something can be done. These pages will give you a specific course of action that, when followed carefully, has resulted in over 75% of interventions concluding successfully.

You will be given the necessary tools to develop an intervention team who will be able to reach the person you are worried about. The process of intervention is based on facts. If drinking or drug use is causing so many problems that it noticeably interferes with a person's life, then you have all the facts you need to act to interrupt the destructive course of the disease.

A Look at the Disease of Addiction

For the purpose of this book, I will frequently describe the use of alcohol. This is done only as a matter of convenience. In the treatment programs that I have been involved in since 1973, the vast majority of the patients have been using more than one drug; although alcohol is usually the drug of choice.

It is also important to remember that when I use the term "alcohol", I am talking about the drug itself, not what it floats in. Very often people try to minimize the impact caused by the alcohol use by suggesting that because they only drink beer, they can't be alcoholics. People become addicted to alcohol regardless of what the alcohol may be in. The alcohol in beer is no different than the alcohol in wine, bourbon or vodka.

Approximately 90% of the liquid medicines in the United States have alcohol in them. The human body cannot tell the difference between the alcohol consumed for medicinal purposes and that consumed for pleasure. The reason for this is simple. Regardless of why the user takes in the alcohol, the body always reacts to the drug in the same way. The type of drug abused or the legality of it are not major factors, because once the disease of addiction is present, the user is actually addicted to all mood-altering drugs.

This also may be an equal opportunity illness. Today more and more women are being diagnosed as suffering from this disease, too.

Today it is being reported that by the fourth grade about 85% of students have experimented with alcohol or other drugs. Some studies suggest that by the time a student reaches the seventh grade, there is a one in five chance that he or she is chemically dependent and in need of treatment.

There are two basic types of addiction. The first is the physical addiction. This is when the body (actually the cells of the body) craves the drug. The second is the psychological addiction. Of the two, psychological addiction is by far the more difficult to treat. That's the issue being faced when people who have "gone on the wagon" for a period of time are now convinced that they have figured out how to handle the problem. While there may be overwhelming evidence *against* the idea of controlled use, they assume it will be safe to return to using alcohol or drugs.

Often a person will claim that since a drug such as cocaine or marijuana is not physically addictive, it can't possibly be a problem. This is not the case. They are both potentially psychologically addictive. This statement just draws attention away from the issues at hand. When this happens, the disease of addiction can continue.

For many years addiction to drugs or alcohol was viewed as a moral weakness. Today we know that this isn't so. The American Medical Association (AMA) issued an opinion in 1957 stating that alcoholism was a disease. We've seen a natural evolution take place with many other similarly misunderstood illnesses. Whether we speak of addiction or epilepsy, we know it's a sickness. And our attitude can make a difference.

To understand this disease better it is important to know how the alcohol and drugs work. Our brains function basically by chemical interaction. If we decide to blink our eyes, there will first be a chemical interaction. If we distort the natural interaction in this sequence by bringing a new chemical into the process, we can still blink but there will be a distortion.

Alcohol is such a chemical. So are tranquilizers, uppers, downers, hallucinogenics, prescribed and street drugs. When a person drinks alcohol, he or she introduces a new chemical into the natural chemical process in the brain. Blinking is still possible when a person is drinking. However, the distortion becomes more and more obvious with the greater level of alcohol consumed.

We see the same effect with other normal physical functions. Frequently when a person has been drinking, this distortion becomes very apparent when they speak.

Memory functions in the same manner. There is a chemical interaction in the brain and we remember what has happened. It is also true that memory will function when a person is drinking or using drugs. But again we see a distortion. The more a person has consumed, the more inaccurate (or distorted) their memory becomes. However, he or she continues to trust these distortions completely, unaware of what is happening.

After several years of facing the denial as well as the aftermath of chemical abuse, it is not unusual for those around the addict or alcoholic to want to throw in the towel. The fact that it is a disease seems to evaporate in thoughts that if addicts or alcoholics really wanted to control their drinking or drug use, they could, that they have no one to blame but themselves.

The irony here is that while a person's lifestyle certainly plays a part, it's only one of several factors. For a comparison, and to help yourself see your feelings on this, ask yourself if you have ever said things like: "Well, he's the one that drinks." "You think she would stop for the childrens' sake." "You have to pay the piper. If you fool around with that stuff, eventually it's going to catch up to you." Now, did you ever make statements like this about a cancer victim? Have you criticized a heart attack patient for not exercising? Probably not. In most cases, all anyone cares about with cancer or heart disease is how to pitch in and help.

The fact that a heart attack victim may have smoked, eaten improperly and never exercised a day in his life does not prevent the heart attack from being viewed as a disease. Neither does the fact that someone may have used chemicals unwisely preclude the results from being a disease.

Reaction to Life-Threatening Diseases

Addiction is a life-threatening disease like cancer or heart disease. It is important to point out that the addicted person has many of the same reactions experienced by the others with potentially fatal illnesses. Usually when a patient is informed that they have such an illness they follow a predictable course that was described in a book entitled *On Death and Dying* by Doctor Elisabeth Kubler-Ross. In her work she says that there are five steps a person will go through in coming to grips with the sickness and in dealing with the emotional trauma the illness causes.

The first step is one of the most natural of all human reactions. This is to deny that the problem exists. Since no one wants to be sick, they deny the presence of any major illness. In most CPR courses, the instructors will address this when they point out that the victim of a heart attack often will tell anyone offering assistance that he is really all right.

The second step is anger. When confronted with the seriousness of the condition, the patient will frequently lash out at the doctor. Often he will tell all within earshot that the doctor is a quack. Should a family member express some feelings, he or she may be attacked for interfering.

When these attempts to get others to not discuss the problem fail, the third step begins. This is negotiating. The cancer patient will plead with God for one more Christmas or a chance to see his or her child grow up. Often these pleas are accompanied by promises to live a new and better life if only they can have one more chance.

The fourth step is depression. As the magnitude of the problem begins to set in, the victim of the illness feels lost and defeated. Eventually they reach a level of acceptance of what is occurring.

With one notable exception, in the disease of addiction we see the same process. The first step of denial is very obvious. Tell a person you think he or she has a drinking or drug problem, and you hear the denial. This is a very natural reaction.

The second step of anger is also predictable. Should you persist in your attempts to discuss the drinking or drug use, you most likely will be attacked. Often the attacks take the form of blaming. Sometimes it is more subtle. If these efforts fail or if you happen to be the person's employer (where yelling would put the individual's job in jeopardy), we will see the third step, negotiations.

More than once a spouse has promised to control drinking or drug use or to stop completely. This has been done with great sincerity and the best of intentions; however, promising to not be sick will not change the sickness.

The next step is depression. All too often a person who suffers from chemical dependency is diagnosed as suffering from clinical depression. The outward signs frequently appear to be the same. This misdiagnosis can be tragic. Clinical depression is often treated with medication. The problem here is that if the diagnosis is addiction and the medication given is potentially addictive, all that occurs is a shifting of the dependency from one drug to another.

The fifth and final step, acceptance, does not usually occur in the victim of chemical dependency without a major outside experience forcing itself on the situation. This is where intervention fits into the picture. Well planned intervention can be just such a "major outside experience" that will confront the addicted person with the reality that his or her chemically affected memory has been distorted and will lead the person toward acceptance of the problem and the solution.

An Overview of the Basic Principles of Intervention

Successful interventions have three key factors. When applied to the best of your ability, you will greatly increase the likelihood of treatment being accepted. These keys are not new and unique to intervention; however, they were a part of any intervention I've ever participated in.

The first key is common sense. When we recognize the impact alcohol and drugs have on a person and their memory, it becomes clear that someone else must act. Waiting for the dependent person to change will not solve the problem. It is also essential to be direct. If the person you are concerned about cannot see how serious the drinking or drug has become, you will need to show him or her.

The second key is honesty. Simply stated, that means identifying specific times when the chemical use was inappropriate or dangerous. This will require careful thought and the recalling of memories that may be painful and that you would rather forget.

The third key may be the most crucial. This is compassion. Without a sincere desire to help, the intervention will not succeed. While your honesty may hold the information the person needs to change, it will be your compassion that will allow him or her to hear it.

There exists today the opinion that a person cannot recover from addiction without first asking for help. In light of the description of addiction used here, we know that this occurrence is rare. Recovery is usually brought on by a series of problems coming together in such a way as to overwhelm the shield.

Today we know that intervention is possible at any stage of the disease of addiction. But as with any major illness, the most desirable time to intervene is when the person who suffers is still early in the disease — in fact, the earlier the better. Rather than waiting for a person to lose his or her health, family, and other reasons for living, the time to act is when the problems begin to stand out.

Ours is a drinking and drug-using society. If someone's drinking or drug use stands out from the norm, do something. You won't have to play doctor. You do not need to diagnose this disease. You will not have to create a problem. All you will need to succeed is a willingness to see what has occurred because of the chemical use and the ability to write that down.

Whether you are just beginning to worry or at the point where the spark of hope is fading, you'll find that with intervention, alcoholism and addiction don't have to win.

2

Understanding Addiction

In order to walk through a general description of the onset of addiction, I will use a man as the victim. Remember, this disease does not discriminate against women. Nor does it care about a person's educational background or social status. The age of the victim is also not relevant.

Ours is an alcohol and drug-oriented society. In any newspaper or magazine, on any television station or billboard, we see ads telling us we can solve our problems, cure ills and even overcome the dreaded "nerdism" if we just use the right chemical. Most children see their parents or other family members drinking from time to time. Celebrities are used to promote the virtues of alcohol. Wishing to be like the grown-ups, kids will imitate what they see.

So with this in mind and to facilitate the story-telling we will use Peter as the name of the person who develops the disease of addiction.

Our friend Peter was like most kids. His family was like most families on their block. He was an average kid in school. Physically he was exposed to the disease of addiction in infancy and childhood through alcohol-based medications.

Environmentally he was exposed when he saw his parents and other adults drinking at parties and by all the advertising and promotion that made alcohol and medications look attractive.

Peter began his drinking and drug use at a high school dance. As the party began, he felt a little shy and awkward. Instead of going out onto the dance floor, he headed out to the school parking lot with his friends. There wasn't a lot of dancing going on in the parking lot. However, there was a lot of "cool" going on there. Since he wanted to be cool, he joined in.

One of his friends had managed to get a bottle from his parents' liquor cabinet. Each boy drank a shot and passed the bottle along. This was Peter's first drink. As he tipped the bottle up and drank, he had pictures of tough movie heroes in his head. He'd seen this done a thousand times in a thousand different television shows and films. But when Peter knocks back his shot, it burns. In fact he's afraid his head might come off. He's still trying to be cool; but his eyes are watering, and he doesn't trust his voice.

There are several conflicting things happening. While the alcohol hurts physically, Peter finds that emotionally it provides him with a warm glow inside. He has a very strong sense of feeling better. As the alcohol reaches his stomach, it is absorbed directly through the lining of the stomach and carried in the blood to the brain. This occurs regardless of having a full stomach or an empty stomach, drinking straight shots or having a beer.

What occurs in Peter's brain is the sedating of the part of the brain that controls his reason, judgment and inhibitions. He can't dance any better after drinking, but he doesn't care. He "feels better".

Our example uses the depressant drug alcohol. However, Peter's first experience may have been with cocaine. Cocaine is a much different drug from alcohol. One is consumed by snorting, injecting or smoking, while the other is consumed by drinking. The alcohol is a depressant, cocaine is a stimulant. The important fact to remember is that regardless of the type or purpose for using the drug, the emotional impact is positive.

For Peter the whole experience has been an emotional uplift. Some time later, after his body has rid itself of the effects of the alcohol, he will once again feel normal. But Peter has just learned that alcohol or other drugs can produce pleasant feelings. The more Peter tries chemicals, the more often he will discover the warm glow. He soon learns that he can control the glow by using certain amounts. He knows that to feel better he has to use more.

He will also learn that if he uses too much of one drug, he can control or modify the impact by using another. Depending on what's available to him, he might use cocaine to get high, then alcohol or some other depressant like Quaaludes to come back down.

Over a period of time early in his drinking and drug use experience, Peter will develop patterns of use and maybe occasional abuse. The patterns are based on his value system. Simply stated, he will not drink or use drugs if it is going to interfere with the things that are important in his life. This is where most social drinkers and recreational drug users are today. While their chemical use may cause an occasional problem, it does not interfere with their normal life responsibilities.

But for Peter things begin to change. These changes are likely to be subtle at first and occur slowly.

Now Peter has gone through college and has got married. He and his wife Gail attend parties on a regular basis. Like most of his friends, he will occasionally overdo it a bit. The first real change in his drinking or drug-using pattern happens at home one evening when he really ties one on. As he is getting ready for bed he falls down, needing help to get up.

When he wakes up the next morning he sees Gail standing at the foot of the bed. He can tell by the look in her eyes that she is upset. Now Peter begins to rationalize the problem. He wants to soothe her feelings of anger and fear, so he looks up with a rather sheepish grin and says, "Ah, Honey, I'm sorry. I don't know what got into me last night. Can you get me a couple of aspirin, please?"

She really does love him. She decides to get the aspirin and some juice to make him feel better. But he is going to hear about this after he has recovered from his hangover.

By the time Gail returns to the bedroom, Peter is sitting up. He smiles at her and says "Boy, I should have known better. You know how I get when I drink on an empty stomach. You did serve dinner a little late last night. And after spending the day in that hot sun doing yard work." Gail hands Peter the aspirin feeling a little guilty for having been mad. She asks him to be a little more careful in the future. Very relieved that the episode is over, Peter promises.

At this point we are beginning to see a trap developing. Gail is relieving Peter of his responsibility for his actions. It's very subtle. The focus was shifted to a late dinner and hot sun as the culprits for his actions. In fact, his actions were the result of his drinking (or drug use). People can get intoxicated on an empty or a full stomach. The chemical used is responsible for intoxication, not food. Once this pattern of the shifting of responsibility begins, there is certain to be further trouble.

For Peter's effort he finds himself with a new and uncomfortable feeling. Even though his chemical use still produces the familiar warm glow, it has now caused him some embarrassment. In the past when the effects wore off, he had returned to his normal feeling of being OK. This time he didn't.

Addiction

For a while, Peter watches his alcohol and drug intake fairly carefully. But a few weeks later he stops off to have a couple of drinks at happy hour with his friends. This time instead of having just two like he planned, he got bombed. This is the beginning of a loss of control for Peter. He does not get drunk every time he drinks, but he is no longer certain what will happen once he starts using alcohol. Some days he can control the use, while on others he can't. This will also happen with drugs other than alcohol. As this happens, Peter finds himself feeling more emotional discomfort. He now feels confused. In other areas of his life he still exercises great control, but not with his drinking or drug use.

The next episode comes when, following a Friday night party, Peter and Gail are in the driveway fighting. She wants the keys to the car. Trying to be funny, he assures her that since he is too drunk to walk, he has to drive. She isn't amused by this but isn't sure what she can do. Gail is too embarrassed to go back into the party and ask a friend for a ride. She doesn't have enough money to take a cab. So she gets into the passenger's side. She is angry, scared and absolutely certain that he is going to hear about this tomorrow.

When tomorrow comes, Peter doesn't get up very early. When he does wake up, he's relieved. He looks around and recognizes that he is at home in bed. His relief fades quickly as he realizes that he doesn't remember how he got there. His last memory was of being at the party.

Understanding the Faulty Memory

Peter has had a blackout, a chemically induced period of amnesia. He did not pass out. He was able to walk, talk and even drive the car home. But his memory did not record these events. It is not uncommon (in the early phase of addiction) to hear people who have experienced a blackout try to minimize the pain by joking about it. They'll say things like, "Wow, I must have had a great time last night. I can't remember a thing."

The evidence of blackouts will usually come up in many intervention-planning sessions. For example, someone might describe a late night telephone call that the addicted person didn't remember the next day. This can trigger a flood of other examples where the loved one's memory was obviously blank. One family had an expression to describe their mother's blackouts. When an episode was noted they would say "Oh well, the lights were on, but no one was home."

A blackout is a very frightening event. It can be so emotionally painful that the unconscious cannot even accept it. When this happens, we see repression. The mind actually blots out the painful memory. It is very subtle, like a fog rolling in over a bay. And it is an unconscious act. Peter does not will this to happen. It occurs. In place of the blank will be an acceptable memory.

Blackouts may seem hard to believe, but they do occur in general medicine as well. A friend of mine who is an Ob-Gyn doctor is only joking a little when he says, "If it weren't for repression (the mind's ability to blot out painful experiences), there would never be any second children."

Since Peter cannot remember last night, his mind takes over and creates a memory for him. As Peter steps into his shower, his thought process is something like this. Peter was at a party last night. At parties people drink or use drugs, so he did. At parties people have a good time, so he did. And after parties, people go home and go to bed. Since this is where he woke up, that's what he must have done. It's logical. It makes sense. So that's his "memory" of the evening. By the time he steps out of the shower, he literally cannot remember that he does not remember last night.

This is not reality. This is Peter's perception of what occurred. He now finds himself thinking that he feels better. Actually, at a very deep level he still feels the terrible fear that the blackout caused. He is just not aware of it.

He heads downstairs with a memory of having had a great time last night and is looking forward to spending the day with the kids. But when he walks into the kitchen and sees Gail, he can tell she is quite upset about something.

She was frightened and hurt last night. Reasonably enough she expects an apology.

For Peter, who doesn't remember the drive home or the fight, the most reasonable thing in the world for him to do is to smile at Gail and say, "Good morning, Honey. Is something wrong?"

Gail can't believe what she is hearing. She screams at him that he has a drinking problem and he had better do something about it.

But Peter doesn't see any evidence of a drinking problem. In fact, all he sees is a wife who nags. He accuses her of being just like her mother. He even suspects that she is trying to turn the children against him.

They may fight back and forth. Or they may grow silent. What is important to point out is that neither Peter nor Gail really understands what is happening. Each feels that the other is being unreasonable. To solve his dilemma, Peter may promise to "go on the wagon". He vows to show her that he doesn't have an alcohol or drug problem by not using for a period of time (the length of time isn't important).

This is an old and time-worn effort to prove that the person is in control. In fact it is a major warning sign that alcoholism or addiction is present. The diagnosis of chemical dependency is based on what occurs when a person is using. Does the use create problems? If so, the alcohol or drug use *is* the problem. Social drinkers seldom need to stop drinking to prove anything since social drinking rarely creates problems.

Physical and Psychological Addiction

As mentioned earlier, there are two distinct types of addiction: physical and psychological. When a physical addiction is present there are several noticeable factors. Most obvious of these is the physical discomfort experienced when a person is abstinent. There may be shakes, excessive perspiring and irritability. And in later stages serious medical problems such as hallucinations are possible. Additional warning signs of a physical addiction include an increase in tolerance. The individual is able to consume greater quantities of a chemical than in the past; in some cases with little or no apparent impact.

The second type of addiction is psychological. Of the two, most experts feel this is the more difficult to treat. A psychological addiction is present when Peter, after having gone on the wagon for a period of time, feels that he can now successfully control his drinking. He believes that by not drinking or using drugs for a period of time he has proved he is in control. Actually, he has only confirmed his psychological addiction when, in spite of overwhelming evidence to the contrary, Peter thinks it is safe for him to drink or use. And the simple fact that he resumes his alcohol or drug use demonstrates his addiction. A successful period of abstinence does not indicate that when Peter drinks or uses again, he will be in control.

What is Peter's attempt to draw attention away from the impact alcohol is having in his life? Emotionally he is experiencing more and more pain. Each new experience creates fear and shame. At some point Peter may begin to sneak drinks. This doesn't necessarily mean that he has a bottle hidden in the toilet tank. To sneak drinks means he is hiding the amount or frequency of his drinking. At parties it may appear that Peter is becoming intoxicated on very little alcohol. However, what the others don't see is that before going to the party, he fortified himself with several drinks.

A person addicted to prescription drugs probably will have in the medicine cabinet bottles of pills from most of the pharmacies located in the surrounding area. Chances are excellent that there will be several doctors (including dentists) prescribing these drugs, none of the doctors knowing about the others. Again, this is an attempt to hide the addiction. It's even possible to find prescriptions for other people in the supply.

If illegal drugs are being used, the shame felt is also great. The need to sneak around to buy a supply, never being sure whether the police will be present or a rip-off taking place, causes a great deal of emotional pain.

As his problems and emotional pain increase, Peter finds it more and more difficult to be close to the people he cares about. He withdraws from them. But because of his drug-affected memory, he can't see accurately that it is he who is withdrawing. He blames those around him.

His family, friends and employer expect Peter to see what his drinking is doing to his life. But he sees his life through his drug-affected memory. He can't see the problems that those around him are talking about. His response is to alter his life so that drinking or drug use is less noticeable but not interfered with.

At this point the progression of the disease of addiction becomes most apparent. While the frequency and quantity of chemical use may increase, what is most noticeable will be the manner in which Peter adjusts his life to his addiction. Rather than curtailing his drinking when it interferes with his life, he alters his life. He drops hobbies that don't allow for drinking.

Peter is less and less able to participate in his own life because of the chemical use. When this happens, others will start to take over his responsibilities. With fewer interruptions to his drinking, his disease will go from bad to worse.

Peter is relying on his distorted memory that tells him he's all right. He finds himself feeling more emotional pain with each passing day. Since he cannot see accurately what is happening to him, he must develop a shield around himself to protect against the pain that he feels. The defenses that he will use to make up his shield will depend on the situation and who is being faced. Peter may use anger, but he can turn around minutes later and be charming.

Because of this odd behavior, the family can't help but get caught into this disease. If you love a person who is suffering, you can't avoid being drawn in. Often this is as subtle as the episode where Peter's wife eased his pain by providing aspirin. Yet with each successive attempt to cover up or ease the immediate problem, the situation grows more painful for the addicted person and those around him.

It's 10 o'clock Monday morning, and Peter is in bed with a hangover. He was expected at work by eight. Since Gail saw there was no way he could make it, she called the boss. She told him that the water heater exploded and that Peter would be in at one. Her natural desire is to be helpful and to protect Peter. When she called the boss, she was trying to be helpful. In fact what she has done is become a part of Peter's shield. She stood between Peter and the problem. When he wakes up Monday and realizes that he didn't get to work on time, he will feel guilty. But since Gail shielded him, he can't see any problem.

When a chemically dependent person is protected from

the problems the drinking or drug use cause, the abuser cannot see any connection between the two.

For Peter, added to his feeling of guilt is the feeling of inadequacy. He's an adult being treated like a child and he resents it. Even if he had asked his wife to cover for him, he would resent it.

Peter feels a welling up of emotional pain. He is also using his drug-affected memory to tell him he's all right. Since he cannot see through his wife's shield, and he has a drug-affected memory that tells him he's all right, he lashes out at his wife. He blames her for his being late for work. If she could only set an alarm clock like any normal person, he wouldn't be late.

Of course Gail is upset. She thought she was being helpful. But rather than being grateful, he yelled at her. Now Gail feels confused, hurt and angry.

Now the disease has progressed to the point where Peter has lost the ability to feel the old glow. What he experiences now is constant internal nagging and emotional pain. His memory tells him that the good old days are still his to have. If everyone would just get off his back, he'd be all right. All he has to do is drink or use drugs and somehow he'll get back the good feelings.

For Peter, relief comes only when he drinks or uses. This gives him a temporary escape from the pain. When he uses, he feels normal. Sober he feels pain, and his drug-affected memory tells him that chemicals will solve the problems. If you suggest to him that this conclusion is wrong, he will question your sanity. Drugs and alcohol seem like friends. They relieve pain.

Each family member and friend takes an active role by trying to protect. Family members will make small adjustments in their lives to ease the pain or tension that they see.

To step back from Peter's and Gail's life and take an objective look, we would see many signs that addiction is present. Peter's physical condition will begin to suffer. His doctor finds high blood pressure, insomnia, gastritis and possibly even border-line diabetes. The marriage that once seemed rock solid now feels like a shell. They've lost their ability to share special quiet moments. The family's social life has slowly diminished, and the children are scared.

It's also important to recognize that we have not discussed the amount, the frequency, or what type of chemical used to reach this point. These are smoke screens. The only issue at hand is whether or not the use of alcohol (in any form) or other drugs is interfering with the person's life.

3

Enabling: How Being Helpful May Hurt

When Peter's wife called his boss and made excuses for his absence, she was enabling Peter in his chemical dependency. Enabling is a term that refers to the efforts of someone to "help" the addict or alcoholic. This is usually done by covering up, by protecting, shielding or in some way easing the immediate problems created by drinking or drug use.

These efforts are meant to help. But they actually kill the chemically dependent person with kindness. Each time Peter is shielded from taking responsibility or being held accountable for the consequences of his drinking or drug use, he is free to continue his chemical use. However, by the next day when he is sober, the crisis has been resolved for him.

The enabling being done on Peter's behalf makes it impossible for him to see any need to change. His drug-affected memory supplies him with an inaccurate picture of what has happened. Coupled with this is the enabling behavior that was intended to help. By covering up, the enabler has placed a shield between the problem and Peter.

And once the shield was placed between Peter and his actions, all Peter can see is the person that placed the shield.

He feels emotional pain but can't connect it to chemical use. What remains for Peter is the awareness that when he is in pain all he needs to do is to drink or use drugs to take him back to "the good old days."

Fear of the Chemically Dependent Person

All too often family and friends get into the enabling trap because they are afraid to confront the chemically dependent person with the facts of his or her dependency. This fear comes from several different areas.

While all of the concerns seem valid, when looked at closely they lose a great deal of their power.

First, experience has shown that when they have tried to have a rational discussion on drinking or drug use with the dependent person, the reaction was unpleasant or disappointing. Sometimes the reaction seemed charming; sometimes the reaction was angry. But whether they faced a sorrowful, tearful person who was promising to change, or a person who acted as if he or she didn't care, one thing remained constant. Nothing changed for the better in the long run.

At this point we must accept that any attempt at a rational discussion is not likely to produce positive change. The disease of addiction presents both the natural denial of the sickness as well as the chemically induced "pleasant" memory that tells the user that nothing is wrong.

Another common fear is that if the dependent people are confronted with their behavior, they will react by getting intoxicated. But, in fact, the disease itself dictates when someone becomes intoxicated. With time and a careful review of past experiences, you will find that whether you say something or say nothing, do something or do nothing, the individual always seems to end up intoxicated. This is because they have the disease of addiction.

Addicts and alcoholics use the ability to manipulate others as a component of their disease. Frequently they have others feeling completely responsible for the illness. But ask yourself this, "Can I cause someone to *have* the disease of cancer?"

If your answer is no, then it becomes reasonable to assume that you cannot cause any other major illness. Since you cannot cause cancer, you cannot cause addiction.

The third area of concern voiced by friends and families is an issue that warrants serious consideration. Many people fear that if something is said or done to confront chemical abusers, they may harm themselves or others. In most cases this is emotional blackmail used by the addict or alcoholic. It is an attempt to get those around them not to act and to distract attention from the chemical dependency.

The possibility does exist that they may try to harm himself or herself. Certainly if there is a history of violence or suicide attempts, you should work with a professional to guide you in your intervention. But your intervention should proceed. What must be considered is that if nothing is done to prevent the natural course of addiction from being run, the outcome is most certainly going to be a premature death. One of the most obvious means by which this can happen is by driving under the influence of alcohol or drugs.

If the potential for self-inflicted harm is so great that you feel it presents a real and immediate threat of danger, I suggest you contact your local mental health service immediately. Share this book with them. Let them know that you want to proceed in the safest manner possible.

Another common fear is that the chemically dependent person is quite fragile and could not "handle" any confrontation. This thought loses its influence when we consider all that they have survived through the years. It becomes meaningless when we consider where the progression of the illness is taking them.

In all of the defenses named (and the million or so others that are used by chemically dependent people), there is one common feature. This feature has been given a wide variety of names, including:

- The no-talk rule
- The code of silence
- The conspiracy of silence

Regardless of what they are called, each defense, each action, is designed to ensure that when the topic of conversation turns to the user's alcohol or drug problems, the flow of discussion is altered and interrupted. Eventually, when there is any discussion of the chemical use, the disruptions become so complete that those around the user stop talking about it altogether.

When this becomes the norm, the enabling process is complete. We now see an individual who is suffering from a disease that he or she cannot see. Those around the victim can see what's happening but are unable to penetrate the absolute shield that the chemically dependent person has built around himself or herself.

As a family member or friend, the more you care for the individual, the more likely it is that you will be drawn into this trap of enabling. Then the disease of addiction becomes as painful for the enablers as it is for the person that has the addiction.

In Peter's story we saw that when he was late for work on Monday morning, he found himself feeling guilty. He wasn't living up to his own standards. When Gail called the boss to cover for him, she, too, compromised her standards. Her reason for doing this is understandable. She fears that if the boss knew the truth, Peter might lose his job and this thought terrifies her. The possibility of this happening on top of all the other problems they are having is just too much.

Even though her reasoning seems to make sense, what actually happens is this. When she protected Peter, she lied. This action caused her to feel guilty. She is also treating her husband as if he were a child. By calling up the boss and covering up she is acting like mommy writing a note to a teacher and she resents this. She is feeling a great deal of fear because she can see that the future she once thought she had is fading away.

After her call when she thought Peter would at least thank her, she found herself hurt and confused. He took all of the pent-up feelings of guilt and shame and threw them at her. He actually blamed her for his problems. His actions were predictable. When Gail stepped between Peter and his problems, she became the only visible reason for his pain.

A Checklist of Enabling Actions

This is a general list of actions that may have been taken with the intention of being helpful. Each has shielded the addict or alcoholic from having to face the facts about his or her chemical use.

Family members frequently:

* Loan money
* Use drugs or drink with the addicted person
* Try hiding the supply of alcohol and drugs
* Solve or cover up problems caused by intoxication
* Observe the no-talk rule among themselves concerning the impact of the chemical use, hoping that by some miracle the problem will go away by itself

Professionals enable when:

Doctors

* Overlook the fact that alcohol is noticeable on a person's breath during medical appointments
* Prescribe sedative drugs without a complete checkup, refilling prescriptions over the telephone, fail to inquire about other medications being prescribed for the patient by other doctors
* Fail to recognize the symptoms of addiction

Ministers

* Fail to recognize that addiction is a disease that requires special care; pastoral counseling by itself (helpful when recovery has begun) is not sufficient
* Condemn addicted people as having a moral weakness rather than a physical illness

Employers

* Accept poor quality work
* Excuse absenteeism and erratic work hours
* Adjust conferences or other business requirements around the known drinking patterns of the employee

* Excuse drinking or drug abuse behavior with statements like, "Well, she's better drunk than most people are sober."

These are just a few of the many possible enabling behaviors. The three basic topics that seem to be avoided in these and all enabling actions are discussions concerning:

a) alcohol and drugs
b) money
c) anything negative

Eventually everyone is walking around on egg shells, afraid to say or do anything, certain that if peace isn't kept at all cost, the chemically dependent person will explode.

At this point we find that the disease of addiction is in full control of Peter and those around him. The normal course of events would be to watch the addict or alcoholic continue to withdraw from his or her own life. With each successive day the addicted person feels more and more isolated and lonely.

Those people who once were close begin to pull away for their own emotional well-being. We see a person trapped in a life that leaves him or her unable to recognize what is happening, truly unable to see any reason or need to change.

Enabling often appears to be a simple, almost painless means by which you can help the person that you care about. The reality is that *to shield is to kill* with kindness. The intentions are the best in the world. We try to help. In fact we end up withholding the very information the chemically dependent person needs to change.

4

Intervention: The Bridge From Suffering To Surrender

The word "intervention" describes the systematic approach used to break through the shield that a chemically dependent person builds. As we have seen, it is necessary to break through defenses to show the dependent person that treatment is needed. An equally important goal of intervention is to motivate the person to act at once.

Successful interventions are based on three fundamental concepts that provide the framework for a presentation that is most likely to result in the chemically dependent person entering treatment. These keys are:

* **Common Sense:** Since we see clearly what addicted persons cannot see, we must show them.
* **Honesty:** We cannot minimize, cover up or soften what needs to be said. Direct, factual information is vital.

* **Compassion:** This may be the most important of all. Participants in an intervention need to tell an individual something that is very painful and risky in a manner that will preserve the dignity of the suffering, chemically dependent person.

The reason compassion may be the most important has to do with the nature of addiction. The chemically dependent person has developed a sophisticated and complex series of defenses that preclude their recognizing how serious their condition is. In fact it is not uncommon that the actual words of the intervention are forgotten by the chemically dependent person, but what is never forgotten are the feelings that tell them someone still cares. A sense of hope exists because the family hasn't given up.

In one instance where a family had come to me, the intervention was with a dentist. He was a large man physically and had a reputation for running his home with an iron fist. The family was very concerned about his leaving the family should they follow through with an intervention. I recently saw him at the treatment center he went through. Five years later he still expresses his gratitude by providing volunteer services there. I asked him what he remembers the most from his intervention and his answer is one that I have heard many times, "I couldn't believe what I was hearing. But the love I saw on the faces told me I would do anything they wanted."

These three keys, combined with the specific guidelines that will be detailed in the next chapter, are the most powerful and effective tools imaginable. They will allow family and friends to channel love and genuine concern through carefully planned phases to show the dependent person that treatment and recovery are needed and, above all, desirable.

The actual intervention itself will not take long. The preparation might. Remember that while you are eager to act, it is vital to act in a way that will gain the desired results. We do not wish to waste time. However, using time effectively at the planning stage is more important than rushing into an intervention half prepared.

Why Intervention Works

In the earlier chapters we saw how persons who have developed this disease have begun to violate their value systems. They do have a sense of what is right for themselves; yet they find that when they drink or use drugs, their actions go against this. As the disease progresses, chemically dependent people feel an increased sense of emotional pain as their actions compromise their values.

What you will do in the intervention is show the individual how their chemical use has caused them to feel the pain that they are in. You will not have to create a crisis. You simply take the available information about the individual that relates to the alcohol and drug use and replay it for them. You present a list of specific incidents and past actions that are tied directly to the chemical use, and you'll do this in a caring and nonjudgmental fashion. You provide the information that they need to make the decision to seek help. Jay Piper of the McDonald Center, Scripps Memorial Hospital in La Jolla, California, calls this "allowing them the dignity of decision".

When you intervene, you construct a bridge from suffering to surrender to the truth of their situation. You establish a means by which they can escape from the pain and loneliness of their addiction.

Each person who suffers from the disease of addiction is different. The disease itself generally is not. Some people may show many symptoms of chemical dependency while others show only a few. Some will tell any and all within earshot that they enjoy the drinking or the drug use and that they have no intention of ever changing.

The fact of the matter is that no one enjoys living in the midst of the disease of addiction. They may well recall the good old days when drinking and using were fun. They certainly would like to recapture those days. But living in the disease is a terrible experience. My belief and the belief of many others in the field is that suffering alcoholics and addicts are begging to find a way out of their misery in spite of their resistance to change. Intervention answers their plea for help.

What To Expect For Your Efforts

In spite of the addict or alcoholic wanting help, at first the individual will probably resent any actions you may take. Several years ago I trained a family to conduct an intervention with one of their sons. He was 22 at the time. During the intervention the family relied on very specific facts as well as economic leverage to ensure that he entered treatment immediately.

We also began preparing to intervene with a younger brother. Our decision was to intervene two weeks after the first brother entered treatment. This young man knew from talking with his older brother what an intervention was, and that the family was likely to intervene with him as well. Even knowing what his family was thinking about didn't preclude a successful intervention.

When we intervened with the younger son the intervention team included his parents, a girl friend and his employer. Again we used specific facts as the primary motivating factor, as well as economic leverage to ensure that he, too, entered treatment immediately. Several years later while sharing his recovery experiences with a group of recovering alcoholics he made several comments about the intervention. He spoke first of the anger he felt at being confronted with his problem. But he then described his gratitude to his parents and friends for taking the risk that they took.

Now age 26, he is a successful businessman and owns his own company. His family's intervention saved him from losing everything he had wanted. It gave him the opportunity to develop into the person he could become.

The majority of individuals will enter treatment immediately following the intervention. They most probably will be feeling a wide variety of emotions: anger, resentment, embarrassment, fear, shame and all the other expressions that typify the disease of addiction. You did not cause these feelings. They are there as a direct result of the chemical dependency.

It is important to remember that regardless of why the person you are concerned about enters treatment, as long as they are in treatment, recovery can begin. Over the years I have heard many dependent people say that they were only entering treatment to shut someone up or to get the boss off their back. I've even heard people say that they would go into a recovery program but planned to return to drinking or using. These are common reactions. They are also meaningless for the most part as they represent the disease talking prior to treatment.

Remember, it is not important *why* people enter a recovery program, only that they do enter one. They stand a far greater chance for recovery in a treatment center than they do sitting in a bar or hanging around their circle of friends who are still drinking or using. The attitude they have when they enter treatment will disappear. The only important attitude is the one they have when they leave treatment.

5

Intervention Strategies: How To Prepare

Interventions are not as difficult as they may seem. Usually when people plan an intervention, they imagine that whatever can go wrong will go wrong. No matter what they try to do, no matter what is said, it won't help. Years of experience have shown me that these suspicions for the most part are unfounded. A carefully planned intervention can work very well, even if something unexpected happens during the process. Any fear or apprehension you feel now is OK. You get to feel anything you like. Fear is normal, natural and healthy. Without it, people would do some very foolish things. Your sense of fear now is a benefit and you can use it to your advantage. It will assist you in preparing for this intervention by encouraging you to cover all the bases and not take anything for granted. The more prepared you are in advance of the intervention, the easier it will be when you actually sit down to intervene.

I strongly recommend that as the preparations are taking place the individual be kept aware of what is happening in a general way. He or she will not need all of the details. But by stating that there is a group concerned about the person's chemical use and that you are learning about what your options are, you help the individual prepare for change. Also mention that at some point the group would like to speak with him or her about these concerns. Don't be discouraged if the individual does not seem cooperative at first. He or she may say no. The answer might be "Never". Don't worry. In the end he or she will hear what you say.

This initial action will serve a couple of useful purposes. Most important is that you start to break the no-talk rules. It also helps the individual start the process of change. Remember, you are planting a seed with this effort. And while the person you are worried about may seem totally unwilling, when you break this no-talk rule, he or she will begin to feel the discomfort caused by the chemical use. No longer is the shield as effective at blocking out the negative effects of drinking or drug use and the fact that others are aware of these effects.

The exception to this recommendation comes if you fear the possibility of domestic violence. In a situation where violence is a possibility, it is best to use a professional to guide you through the actual intervention. Quite possibly a clergy member or physician may be available to help.

If you find yourself in this category you will follow all of the other preparation steps but you *will not* discuss your gathering of information. Also before the intervention, find out where the closest program for battered persons is. Make arrangements to and plan to go to them for a place to protect yourself if the intervention doesn't end with the person you are worried about going to treatment immediately.

Who Can Help

Step one is the identification of all those people who from their own experience with the chemically dependent person could list specific negative or harmful incidents directly related to the victim's drug or alcohol abuse. This list of who might contribute includes:

- family members
- friends

* employer, co-workers or company employee assistance counselors
* clergy
* medical personnel
* professional therapists
* probation officers

There is no ideal number of people to participate in an intervention. Two may be better than one; some teams have had as many as twenty-two. The ideal size is that number of people who care enough to risk being involved and who have examples that support their concern. The intervention team can include virtually anyone who is willing and who can cite specific personal experiences that directly relates to the individual's drinking or drug use.

The intervention where twenty-two people were present was very time-consuming to develop. All but two people present were immediate family members or spouses. The decision to use a group this large was based on our need to intervene on both a husband and wife. We felt that an overwhelming picture was required to penetrate the shields that the couple had built over many years of drinking together.

People often wonder whether children should participate. In most cases, the kids know as much about the sickness as anyone. Including the child as a part of the recovery can be a very positive experience. Consideration should be given to the age of the children who may be involved and their ability and willingness to describe what for them are very painful memories. As a rule of thumb, I seldom include children under ten.

Sometimes an exception to this is appropriate. In one family when we were intervening with a teenager, it proved to be the best tool we had. In this case, a five-year-old brother meant the difference between success and failure. During the course of the intervention the seventeen-year-old boy was stretched out in his chair, chewing gum just loud enough to be distracting and appeared to block out everything being said. His parents pointed out that with the way things were going, he wouldn't be able to go to college. This was a kid who was flunking gym. College was probably not a priority in his set of values. The examples being cited meant very little to him. The presenters were addressing their own value systems, not his. Finally his younger brother looked at him and said, "Billy, I saw you steal money out of my piggy-bank to buy your drugs. You lied to me and said that you didn't. But I know that you did, and I don't want you to be my big brother until you quit." This proved to be what was required. Billy went into treatment. A significant part of his value system was to be the big brother. When he realized he wasn't because of his drug use, he faced reality and accepted help. The point here is that anyone can participate.

To decide who shouldn't be in an intervention is equally important and usually more difficult. Some people, for whatever reason, are so angry that they cannot set their anger aside long enough to be able to share with the addicted person in a caring and non-judgmental fashion. They should not sit in on the intervention. However, they might be willing and able to participate in the preparation.

Others who may not suit your purposes are people who in spite of the overwhelming evidence of addiction, refuse to see it. This is their right. Attacking them will not help. Offer them the chance to sit in on the training if they would like, but don't try and force them into acting.

The last group that should be avoided if at all possible will be those who are actively addicted themselves or are suppliers of alcohol and drugs to the person you plan to intervene with.

I have set up interventions with participants who themselves are addicted and even one situation where the drug dealer actually participated. Obviously these were less than ideal circumstances.

In the case where we used the drug supplier, the intervention came about in an abrupt fashion. While on a business trip I was called at my hotel and asked if I would meet with a group of people that wanted to set up an intervention. We met in a restaurant and planned the intervention. Normally I would take six to eight hours to prepare a family. In this instance we only took about two hours. I hadn't yet got a clear picture in my mind of who each of the team members were. But when confronted during the intervention, the individual said that if his own supplier thought he needed help, he had better get it.

I hadn't known that his supplier was there. If I had, I would have asked him to leave. I recommend against using these people because their history has been one of actively supporting the disease. While they may really want to be helpful, it is difficult to risk the potential damage they might cause. This damage might include disrupting the flow of information during the intervention or attempting to minimize the impact the chemical use has had in the individual's life.

The first step in getting ready is to sit down and draft a list of persons who may be able to contribute. I suggest that you actually write out this list (and all other lists that you will be told about while you prepare) and include every potential name. Do not cheat yourself by deciding for them. When you are dealing with other adults, let them be responsible for their own actions. All too often potentially valuable participants don't help because they are not asked. Someone will decide that "they would never help" so no one approaches them.

People who live out of state are often excluded from consideration. These might be close family members, kids in college or long-time family friends. They should be included on the list. Their actual participation may be limited to sending a tape recording of their concerns or providing a letter to be read by one of the other participants. If they have information to share with the user, they should be invited to participate in any way they can.

Step two: Once you have written out your list of names, contact those people. Talk to them face to face if at all possible. You'll want to say something like, "Cathy, lately I've become very worried about Peter's drinking (or drug use). I am thinking of gathering a group that cares for him and is as concerned as I am. I was wondering if you'd be willing to come to an initial planning session to see if there is enough concern to act?" Explain to the potential team member that your plan calls for a group of concerned people sitting together to use love and facts to show the person you are worried about why you think he or she needs help.

It is helpful to point out to people who may be somewhat hesitant to join in that at this point you are only asking for them to be a part of the preparation. Before the actual intervention, they may decide they don't want to participate. Try to be understanding if this happens. Tell them that this is all right. You're just asking them to get the facts. The final decision is up to them. But they can't make an intelligent decision unless they are informed.

Step three: Once the core group is formed, you can begin with your planning. In your initial meeting you should inform the group of the basic nature of the disease of addiction. Use the information in the front of the book to point out that because of the impact of alcohol and drugs on the victim's memory, it is vital to show clearly the facts of his or her behavior.

List-making Techniques

Explain that to do this each person must write out a list of specific examples. These must be tied directly to chemical abuse. It may be very aggravating when a person leaves clothes on the bathroom floor. But unless a bottle of whiskey or some other drug is in the pile, the incident would not be relevant to your intervention. This is not to be a general gripe session but a demonstration of how the person's behavior under the influence of drugs and alcohol is creating pain and chaos in his or her life and is alienating loved ones.

There are three reasons to have each participant write out a list. First, during the intervention anxiety levels usually go way up. When this happens, memories tend to be blocked out. Having a written list ensures that you will not leave out important points that you want to make.

Second, when you take the time to write out the list, you show at a very deep level that you care. You are not shooting from the lip; you are prepared.

The final reason to have a written list is that as a component of your intervention, you will ask the person you are concerned about to agree to sit and listen without interruption. Even when the person agrees to do this, he or she may still try to manipulate the group nonverbally. They can stare and scare or start to cry and make you want to stop the intervention. If they begin to do this, you'll have a place to focus your eyes. You will not have to get into a staring contest or be distracted by other manipulative actions.

If some participants are unwilling to take the time and effort to write a list, you might seriously consider not using them.

Writing out your lists is very important to the success of the intervention. Frequently, people who are preparing for an intervention will say something like, "I know a million things that could be written." However, thinking of specific examples and presenting them effectively is vital and generally is not that simple.

Since the examples must be specific, here are several areas to review. I suggest that the intervention group do some brainstorming since this usually helps stir everybody's memory. Areas to be examined include:

1. **Changes in the pattern of drinking or drug taking,** such as:

a) *increase in amount consumed*

Often in the early stages of addiction the ability to drink greater amounts or use more drugs than others is portrayed as a symbol of "toughness", where later the person becomes very defensive about how much they drink or use.

b) *denial of drinking or using when it is obvious that the person has been*

It is not uncommon to smell alcohol on the breath of someone even as they stand before you and deny having had anything to drink. Attempts to hide this are noticeable when the person uses excessive aftershave lotion, perfume or breath mints.

c) *hiding the frequency or amount consumed*

Often seen when prior to leaving for a party, the person begins drinking or using.

d) *broken promises and attempts to quit or moderate*
This often takes the form of switching to "a less hard" drug or drink, such as from whiskey to beer, or cocaine to pot. It may also be a stated period of total abstinence.

2. **Changes in personality,** such as:
   a) *angry outbursts for no apparent reason*
   Yelling at people or accusing them of being against him. May include irrational statements about fidelity, finances or other potentially volatile topics.
   b) *violent outburst*
   Physically lashing out at objects such as doors and walls.
   c) *silly or irrational actions*
   Tearing up currency while intoxicated or buying expensive gifts as a means to apologize.
   d) *by comparison how does the intoxicated behavior differ from his or her sober actions*
3. **More frequent health problems,** such as:
   a) unexplained broken bones or bruises
   b) frequent complaints of stomach problems
   c) blackouts (chemically induced amnesia)
   d) depression
   e) use of multiple doctors and dentists to obtain drugs
   f) use of several pharmacies to fill prescriptions in order to hide dependency
4. **Episodes of legal problems,** such as:
   a) arrests for driving under the influence
   b) stealing to support the disease of chemical dependency
   c) financial problems
5. **Disruptions in normal activities,** such as:
   a) giving up hobbies or other activities that either don't include or interfere with drinking and drug use.
   b) a significant drop in grades at school
   c) loss of jobs
   d) loss of usual social circle in favor of drinking and using friends

6. **Disruptive occurrences on special occasions,** such as:
   a) Christmas
   b) birthdays
   c) Thanksgiving
   d) anniversaries
   e) parties

These are just a few of the areas that you might look at. There may well be numerous other experiences that you recall. It is important to remember that, as each member of your group goes through this process, you will relive some of the emotional pain that the episode had caused you. Because of this, it is especially important to try to be as supportive of and gentle with each other as you can be.

Writing the List

To have the maximum impact the list has to be written to express *why* you are concerned. To achieve this each example used should include:

a) the approximate time and date of the incident
b) who was present
c) where the episode took place
d) amount and frequency of drug or alcohol use, and the person's actions after the use (for example slurred speech and staggered gait)
e) a description of how you felt as an observer. Remember to describe a *feeling* (such as "hurt," or "scared,"). *DO NOT JUDGE.*

For example, "Last Christmas Eve you began drinking at two in the afternoon. You said you would only have a couple, take a nap and go to midnight services. By six o'clock you had so much to drink, you were unable to walk straight. You fell into the Christmas tree and knocked it over. I was angry and hurt. But what really scared me was that the next day when you woke up, you couldn't remember any of it."

By tieing together the variety of experiences like this one, you show why you believe the addicted person needs help.

Since family members often share the same experiences, some of the information on lists will be the same. This is all right. Each person will have his or her own feelings about what took place.

There is no set number of items for each list. Obviously, if you find that you are writing a novel, you may want to eliminate some of the material. But before dropping any examples, I recommend that you discuss it with the other group members. You will get a chance to do this in the dress rehearsal prior to the actual intervention.

The examples should be written to show the progression of the disease as reflected in the person's actions. Each participant should cite the oldest incidents first. These should be the first time drinking or drug use stood out in your memory as being uncomfortable. The list should then move towards the most recent.

After all the lists are completed, the group should sit together and conduct a mock intervention. This means that each person in the group will present his or her list as if the person that you are worried about is sitting there.

The purpose of this practice session is to ensure that the lists contain specific examples that deal only with the individual's chemical use and that the lists are presented in a caring and non-judgmental manner that is likely to be heard.

In the Christmas Eve example just cited, the original presentation during the rehearsal was very harsh and judgmental. The spouse accused the drinker of ruining everyone's holiday and being a drunk. She had even expected that he would remember having toppled the tree. Naturally she had felt hurt and angry. And while her original statement may seem true, it is important to remember that the purpose of the intervention is to get help for the sick person. If he or she is attacked or judged, it lessens the chance of a favorable response to your intervention.

Each participant should listen carefully to what the others say. Often they will be made aware of problems that they did not know existed. They also will be able to hear any judgmental statements. It is possible to take any statement, no matter how harsh, and make it a positive and usable example.

The best way to achieve the honest and nonjudgmental tone you want is to write the list as if it were being presented to you. Does your list contain the facts that you would need to see the problem? How do you feel about the way it sounds when you are the person being intervened upon?

As the lists take shape the next step is for each member to write a letter that describes how he or she feels about the individual. This letter will actually be used as the opening statement by each participant. This should be brief. In your letter you should tell the person that you care about him or her, and that's why you are there. The idea is to describe how you feel about this person aside from the disease of addiction. You may even take the opportunity to discuss your need to do this.

As a means to alleviate any fear you may be experiencing, you may even include a statement about realizing you might be risking your relationship. However, your sense of concern is so great you feel you must say what is on your list.

Immediately following this letter of concern, the presenter then describes in detail the examples that are on his or her list. After each person has presented the letter of concern and the list of incidents, the presentation concludes with a request for the individual to get help.

A condensed example of one presentation might be something like this: "Peter, I'm here today because we've been close friends for many years. And quite frankly when Gail told me her concerns about your drinking and that she wanted me to help her talk with you, well, my first thought was that I might be losing a friend who has been like a brother to me. So even though you may get mad, I'm here today because I do care, and I want my friend back.

"I first noticed that your drinking was changing about three years ago. Several of us went on a two-week fishing trip. We had a little rain and rather than going out, you began to drink beer. During the rest of the trip you made several trips to the store for more beer. But what bothered me the most is that you didn't go out on the lake once.

"The next time was at Cathy's birthday party two years ago. We had a barbecue with several couples from around the block. By early evening you had had so much to drink that you sat in the kitchen talking to yourself. I remember feeling embarrassed. I carried you home after the party and took you upstairs. You were unable to get undressed. The next morning when I said something to you about what had happened, you stared at me with total disbelief. You even assured me that you had been the life of the party.

"Because of these things that keep happening when you drink, I want you to get help. I know you're a loving husband and father, but I've seen you drive with your family in the car when you could barely walk because you had been drinking. You're not the type of man who would hurt his family. But the drinking has got so bad now, it could happen.

"For your sake, and your family, I hope you go for help today."

Certainly most lists will contain more information than this example, but this should give you a picture of how the material will be presented.

There are several different techniques that may assist you in your intervention. Since the chemically dependent person relies heavily on a drug-affected memory, it is imperative that we show the strongest possible proof that chemical use is interfering. In several interventions family members have obtained a tape recording (occasionally a video tape) of the person while intoxicated. The family members then used these tapes to show how the person actually sounds and acts.

In one instance I trained a woman to intervene even though she had no one else to participate. Her husband was an alcoholic who had successfully hidden his illness. To convey her concern she relied on two very powerful tools. He took great pride in his penmanship yet when he drank, his handwriting quickly became a blur. After presenting numerous examples from memory to her husband, he still denied that any problem existed. To set aside his shield she produced a series of checks he had written in a local bar. She pointed out that the first check was always neatly written and recorded in the register. Subsequent checks, however, were sloppy, difficult to read and only occasionally entered into the register.

He looked at the checks and still denied any problem. She began to describe the conversation they had had the evening before. At that point he became angry and stated that he was sober the night before. She was just over-reacting to his having a few drinks to relax. She then pulled a cassette tape machine from her purse. She said, "I know you think you were sober last night. But I want you to hear what you really sounded like." She played the tape for him. His voice was recognizable but from his speech it was clear he had been highly intoxicated. Her thinking to tape-record the evening before the intervention proved to be the needed lift for her intervention to reach her husband. He entered treatment.

In some situations it may not be possible for someone who wants to participate to be physically present. In instances like this it may be appropriate for that person to review the list of concerns with the group over the telephone, then record it on a cassette. The cassette then can be played during the intervention. If a tape recorder isn't readily available, a letter might be sent and then read by the group spokesperson.

6

Treatment Options

The last stage of the intervention will require identifying the treatment program you would like to see attended. To select the proper level of treatment will require a basic understanding of the types of treatment available. The options available include both inpatient and outpatient care.

Not all chemically dependent persons require hospitalization. Those who do usually are in an advanced state of the disease. This is noticeable by multiple health problems. These warning signs would include problems such as:

- withdrawal symptoms when drinking or drug use is stopped
- a history of high blood pressure or heart disease
- a jaundiced or yellow pallor of the skin
- known liver problems

Solicit advice from the individual's doctor concerning possible treatment options whenever possible.

Inpatient care is recommended if the individual is living in an unhealthy or nonsupportive environment where the likelihood of staying sober in an outpatient program is poor.

Some of the factors that would weigh against outpatient services include:

* living with people who abuse chemicals
* currently unemployed or with a large amount of unstructured time each day
* no recent history of abstinence

Regardless of whether the group has decided on inpatient or outpatient care as the best alternative, the treatment center should be selected with a great deal of care. I strongly recommend that you arrange an appointment with the facility's program director or medical director. There are specific components that should be fundamental in the treatment service. These include:

* a medical checkup upon entering the program
* a medical plan for the detoxification of the person you are worried about
* family care that has the family participating in counseling, educational and self-help groups.
* a clearly written schedule of activities that combine education, group and individual counseling, as well as physical fitness activities
* aftercare (is there a structured, on-going program following treatment that includes the patient and family?)

Experience has shown that these are important elements in recovery, and family members participating in treatment increase the chances for a successful recovery. Other important concerns that should be raised include the treatment center's integrity in care. Area physicians may be able to give referrals that will be appropriate.

I suggest that you ask the following question. "Will you admit for detoxification only?" If they say "yes", run out of there as fast as you can. Detoxification is the medical management of withdrawal symptoms and is only a small part of treatment. Simply removing alcohol and drugs from the chemically dependent person is no more effective than going on the wagon. To detoxify only would be a form of enabling. Just sobering a person up will not treat this disease. Any center that practices this form of enabling should be avoided.

Your goal is to find the center that will provide the best quality of care. From my experience, this requires a complete program plan.

By far the most popular and widespread system of inpatient treatment used today is referred to as the "Minnesota" or "Navy" model. These programs rely heavily on a combination of group counseling, education and participation in self-help groups. The basis of these programs is the need for total abstinence from all mood altering drugs such as alcohol (in any form), marijuana, tranquilizers, sleeping pills or others. From this abstinence they build a network of recovery supports. In my experience these programs are the most effective for the majority of chemically dependent people. This is the type of program I recommend whenever possible.

Outpatient care is by far the least expensive and disruptive of all formal treatment systems. This is generally more effective when a person is employed or has some other influential force to monitor his or her progress.

The most effective long term successful treatment in history has come from the self-help group known as Alcoholics Anonymous. This has been copied in several other areas so that there currently exists groups such as Narcotics Anonymous, Emotions Anonymous, Gamblers Anonymous and others. Each of these has a specific role in the recovery cycle.

As an intervention group you will need to discuss and decide what is going to be required. Remember that you are trying to choose a treatment program mostly likely to help the person you are concerned about. A frequent trap family and friends fall into is to assume that the individual they are intervening with will not accept inpatient care even though this is what is needed. As a result the group sets inpatient care as its goal. But at the first sign of resistance the group backs away from the goal willing to accept outpatient care or for that matter anything because it seems better than nothing.

Your goal must be a reasonable plan of action that every member of the group will support. For the full impact of the intervention to be felt, the group will need to be consistent and firm in whatever course is chosen. When there is difficulty in coming to a consensus, don't allow this to sidetrack your group from developing their written material. From my experience this happens when a participant has second thoughts about the intervention. Often this change of heart reflects the participant's basic belief or wish that if the individual really wanted to sincerely stop using alcohol or drugs, he or she could stop without outside help.

This is a normal reaction and one that should not cause great concern. Ask the participant to continue developing the written materials with everyone else. Then with a clearer picture of the severity of the drinking and drug problems, the group can further discuss the treatment goal. If the picture that emerges is one of a long and serious involvement with chemical use, ask the hesitant participant to reconsider the group's goal in light of the overwhelming information that has come out.

During this time you should proceed with plans for whichever treatment program the majority has selected. If the reluctant participant still doesn't follow the group, you may consider asking him or her not to participate in the intervention. If you must do this, remember that it is necessary in order to achieve your goal. You are not passing judgment on this person.

If the group does not show a consistent and firm stance about the best treatment method, you decrease the likelihood of a successful intervention. Remember that the disease will cause the individual to attempt to manipulate the group to avoid treatment. No matter how persuasive or sincere the individual seems, a person with the disease of addiction needs help.

A final note about selecting your treatment goal. I'm often asked about the possibility of a person going to Alcoholics Anonymous meetings on his or her own without attending a formal treatment program. Since Alcoholics Anonymous has the most success long-term in helping alcoholics to recover, the question may seem reasonable. And it may be an acceptable attempt. If as a group you would want to agree to this effort, you would include an alternative action plan in case the first doesn't work out. The alternative action plan would call for the individual to enter treatment immediately if he or she returned to any alcohol or drug use. The group should be prepared to reconvene the intervention to ensure compliance.

Personally, my recommendation is to use a formal treatment program that will send the patients to Alcoholics Anonymous and Narcotics Anonymous meetings while in treatment.

Insurance Coverage

As is the case with most health care today, the cost of treatment may seem high. But many insurance programs will cover all or a part of the cost of care. When the group has finished talking with the different potential treatment centers, ask that center to verify the level of coverage the individual's insurance will provide. Your insurance policy or membership card will usually show a telephone number that can be called to check on the coverage.

In some health care plans there is a specific clause that excludes treatment for chemical dependency. Others, especially the health maintenance organizations, may cover only the period of detoxification, not treatment. The rationale seems to be that treatment costs far too much; and insurance plans are worried that if treatment is readily available, these services may be abused. In spite of this most studies indicate that it costs far less to treat addiction than to leave it untreated. This logic shows that a bias still exists in some areas of health care. Since we cannot change this apparent contradiction, we must look for the best alternatives available.

When the group decides that inpatient care is the only acceptable course, but due to insurance limitations or for other financial considerations the family cannot pay for a local hospital program, you can look for programs outside your community. In several areas around the United States there are excellent treatment centers that do not cost as much as hospital-based programs.

Some years ago I was asked to help conduct an intervention

with a young man from San Diego who was hooked on cocaine and other drugs. The debt created by the addiction was overwhelming the family financially. There was no way he could afford treatment in San Diego. By asking for help from a number of family members, the man's wife raised enough money to pay for treatment and to buy a plane ticket.

Some centers around the country offer less expensive services, usually because the treatment center is not located in a general hospital. It may be on the hospital grounds; but due to licensing and other factors it frequently will cost less.

Another very common option that is available to families begins with a calculation of the cost of addiction. This is done by adding the actual cost of the chemicals to the money lost or spent on legal fees, fines, higher insurance rates, lost days from work and other related expenses. Quick addition shows an annual cost that is very high. Since this money is available to be spent on the addiction, it will be available to spend on recovery once the person is in treatment. Many lending institutions will make loans against collateral, such as a house. The use of a loan is a viable means to get help.

An important consideration before you make a treatment facility selection is to look around the facility carefully. Visit the center if possible or call frequently. Make sure you feel comfortable with the staff. And if at all possible, don't let financial considerations be the determining factor for a choice of treatment programs. Some families have even changed their insurance coverage to get the needed assistance. Work with your chosen center and if possible with your insurance agent.

7

Setting Up The Intervention

Knowing what you want to say is only a part of the intervention. The actual setting up of the intervention is also important. Included in this is to:

a) select someone to act as the spokesperson for the group
b) decide the order of presentation
c) select the time and the place for the intervention
d) discuss what excuses might be used for refusing treatment and work out responses to the refusal
e) establishing the group goal
f) a complete dress rehearsal of all plans, statements and actions by the intervention team members

Each of these areas of preparation is described below. All are important. Once you have made your decision to intervene, these issues should be addressed at the same time you are preparing your examples of concern.

Usually the best spokesperson is the one most likely to be listened to by the addicted person. There is no clear-cut method to decide who this person may be. As a matter of course the spokesperson is normally a member of the group.

However, the use of a minister or other professional is acceptable. Before assuming this role, the spokesperson should read this book and be involved in the preparations.

Employers generally have a great deal of influence, making them strong candidates for acting as spokesperson. Sometimes a family member is better. The group should discuss the subject and agree on the most likely candidate.

The spokesperson has several key functions to complete. First he or she should advise the chemically dependent person early in the group's planning that you are concerned about the chemical use and are seeking information for your own benefit, and you hope to discuss this with him or her at some future time.

Frequently I'm asked if this is a necessary step. My experience shows me that in most cases it is very important to the success of the intervention. While it is not an absolute requirement, it can prevent the guilty thought that you are sneaking around behind the addicted person's back. And by bringing the subject up, you are breaking the no-talk rule that has stifled the family's communications.

You can reasonably expect that the addicted person will not embrace the idea of a meeting. In fact they probably will tell you that they will never meet with you on this subject. That is seldom the case. Usually this is an attempt to reinforce the no-talk rule to avoid facing the problems. Your best response after a refusal would be to simply say that you hope they will reconsider when the time comes.

The next major function of the spokesperson is to direct the flow of the intervention. To better make this point, here's a script of what might be said by the spokesperson at Peter's intervention.

"Thank you for joining us today Peter. As I mentioned to you recently several of us have felt concerned by what we have seen when you drink and use drugs. Because of this I would like to ask you to agree to sit and listen to what each of us has to say without interruption. Will you agree to this?"

"What is this? You just expect me to sit through all of you taking pot shots at me?"

"Peter, I know this isn't easy but believe me no one is here to take pot shots. We're all concerned, and we need to know that you will listen to our concerns. After we're through, there will be time to discuss anything we need to. So does this mean you'll hear us out?"

At this point Peter may nod his head or say something that may sound a little sarcastic, but he has agreed. Now the spokesperson says "Gail, why don't you start."

Once the intervention begins, the spokesperson only steps in (other than to present his or her own material) if the individual tries to interrupt. At this point the person should be reminded of the agreement to sit and listen. The only time I suggest responding to a question is if the individual asks what it is the group wants him to do. If this happens, tell him. Be specific, "We want you to go into treatment immediately. In fact we feel so strongly about this, we've made arrangements for you to go to the center now." If he or she agrees, you go. If he or she balks or wants to argue, simply remind him or her of the agreement to sit and listen and continue the intervention.

The spokesperson also has a major role at the end of the intervention. After all the participants have concluded their lists and each has requested that the individual get help, the spokesperson must explain what the group means by "help". Don't hesitate to be specific. Be prepared to answer questions in a direct manner.

As stated in chapter five, where there is a potential for violence, the planning for intervention will remain the same. The only difference is in how you approach the actual intervention, and what actions you will take if the individual doesn't go to treatment immediately.

After the group has developed all of the material to present during the intervention and has made arrangements for immediate acceptance into treatment, two members of the intervention team should contact the individual and ask him or her to participate in the meeting. Tell the person who you are concerned about that this is a meeting to discuss your feelings about the drinking or drug use. *Do not* negotiate a separate meeting in private or accept an opportunity to speak to the individual alone.

Before actually notifying the individual of the meeting, you should contact the nearest center for battered or abused spouses. You can use the telephone directory to locate this number or call a local church or the local medical society. You won't need to give your name. Simply ask for a referral. Once you have a name and number, call the center immediately. Explain the circumstances of your intervention and that your goal is to assist the person who you are worried about to get professional help.

At the conclusion of the intervention, the goal is to have the individual go immediately into treatment. If he or she does not do this, you should go immediately to the center for your own protection. At that time the staff will help you decide how best to deal with this aspect of your relationship.

Selecting The Time and Place For Your Intervention

It is virtually impossible to intervene when the individual you are worried about is under the influence of drugs or alcohol. With this in mind, it is important to consider when the person is most likely to be sober before you select the time and place for the intervention.

If the individual shows up under the influence, *don't* intervene. Wait for the first available opportunity when they are sober. State your disappointment that even though they had agreed to talk with you about their drinking and using, they didn't follow through with their word. Try not to be harsh or judgmental. Be as matter-of-fact as you can. Then add this episode to your data list: "One of the reasons I'm most worried about you is that even after agreeing to meet and discuss your drinking with us, you were unable to keep sober for our meeting. That's why I feel you need professional help."

It may be a little better if you can catch the person with a hangover. Their natural defenses are lower. If they are abusing prescribed medicines, you may not be able to wait for them to be free of the drug effects. In this case, time your intervention to be on or before they take the second dose for the day or when they are most like "normal".

The site for the intervention should be one that is away from the individual's normal home ground. Using the individual's office or home places him or her in a role of being in charge. You want the person to listen during the intervention, not direct it. If at all possible, use a neutral location. If you are working with a health care professional, minister or an intervention counselor from your local treatment center, it may be best to use his or her office. If you would prefer to work with an intervention counselor but cannot find one locally, check the Resources listed at the back of this book.

Occasionally it may be necessary to change the site or time of the intervention. If this happens, remember that your goal is still treatment for the person you are worried about. If some flexibility on your part will make achieving your goal possible without enabling the disease, be flexible.

Order of Presentation and the Intervention Process

When trying to decide the order of presentation, the potential impact of the material should be the guide. The group should determine the two people who have the most powerfully persuasive information on their lists. One of these two, the one with the strongest hand to play, should go first. The other person should go last and reiterate the sense of urgency that the group feels. Often I have found that having a child speak last, especially the youngest child, can show just how much pain the family feels and how far the situation has progressed.

The remainder of the order of presentation is not as important. Most groups have a natural sense of how this should be handled.

How the Intervention Will Look

Before the actual intervention takes place the group should completely walk through each phase of the preparations. This will include reviewing the goal and each of the details. Once the group is comfortable with the plans a dress rehearsal should be conducted. During this rehearsal one of the group members may act as the chemically dependent person. The group must listen carefully to ensure that the material being presented is specific and caring.

The spokesperson will inform the individual of when and where you are meeting for the intervention to discuss the drinking and drug use. Since the likely initial reaction is a refusal to attend, it is best to ask the individual a few days in advance. This allows time for the message to sink in that you are serious about discussing this issue.

The interveners should be at the site before the individual. Whenever possible, the spokesperson should arrange to bring the individual to the intervention.

The room should be set up in a circle. As the individual enters the room the spokesperson should take control of the situation immediately. He or she does this by directing the individual to the empty seat. The empty seat should be the seat farthest from the door. The spokesperson will then briefly state something to the effect that the reason everyone has come together is because of their concern about the chemical use. At this point the spokesperson will ask the individual to agree to sit and listen without interruption. As stated earlier this is done with the understanding that there will be time for discussion after the group is through. Remember that once this agreement is made, never ask the individual a question. Not even a rhetorical question, such as; "Do you remember the party last Friday night?" These questions open the floor to discussion and at the same time imply that the individual's memory is good enough to recall accurately the impact the chemicals are having. If this were the case, you wouldn't need to intervene.

The person who sits next to the individual or across from him or her is not crucial. However, when possible, it's always a good idea to have someone who is very important in the life of the individual sitting directly across from him or her.

The use of physical force to get a person to the intervention or keep them in the room once the intervention has begun is seldom effective.

If the person refuses to attend the meeting, the group should meet as scheduled. The immediate goal then is to decide where and when the group can reconvene the intervention. In one instance a family planned an intervention with a woman in her early fifties. She refused to attend so the family decided that the only way she was likely to hear their concerns was if they went to her. They planned to conduct their intervention in the living room. But she refused to leave her bedroom. Finally after waiting for a short period of time, the family trooped down the hall, entered her bedroom and conducted the intervention there.

The point here is that even if the first strategy doesn't work exactly as planned, other options remain open. This family succeeded in large part because they wouldn't take no for an answer.

Once the spokesperson begins and the agreement to sit and listen is made, the intervention will usually go quickly. The first presenter reads his or her letter of concern and proceeds directly to the lists of examples and concludes by asking the individual to get help.

As soon as the first presenter is through, the second begins following the same format. This is done until all presenters have said what they wanted to say.

The phrase "reading their" list does not necessarily mean literally reading word-for-word from the list. Some people find this to be easiest and least painful. Others may rely on the list as an outline only. Whichever style is most comfortable is acceptable.

The spokesperson then concludes by discussing what the group wants. This should be a direct statement that identifies the treatment center the group identified.

One extra suggestion, which isn't critical but may be of value, is to have a few boxes of tissues handy. Then if someone begins to cry, the intervention isn't interrupted by people chasing all over for something to wipe their eyes.

Overcoming Objections

I suspect that there may be endless reasons why people could offer for not being able to go into a treatment program. *Remember that not one of them is valid.* If a victim of cancer were to state that he or she couldn't afford to take the time off from work or school to get help, you wouldn't accept that excuse. Chemical dependency is just as deadly as cancer if left untreated, and there can be no valid reason for refusing help.

I once had a man assure me that because he was a salesman he had to drink. There was no way he could afford to stop. While to some people that may sound reasonable, imagine a diabetic saying, "I have to eat sugar because I'm a salesman. My customers expect it." No one has to drink to keep a job. In fact a person's drinking may eventually cost him or her a job.

Others state that an admission of their dependency problem would ruin a reputation they have built over the years. This is a real fear for many people. For example, a pilot might fear the loss of a medical certificate which would cost him his job. Doctors and nurses are often fearful if they know they must cooperate in a diversion program in order to maintain their licenses. These fears are real to the individual. They cannot be ignored. But neither can they be accepted. The alternative to successful treatment is death, and the time preceding that death is filled with a great deal of loneliness and misery. The consequences of leaving the chemical dependency untreated are far to great too permit the group to accept any excuses. And the possible loss of a job is highly unlikely if treatment is accepted since treatment is provided under strict federal laws concerning confidentiality.

Each member of the intervention group should list excuses that might be used by the dependent person and then plan an effective answer.

Also keep in mind that just because an intervention doesn't follow the exact plan that is laid out, it doesn't mean it didn't work.

I once was working with a family, preparing them to do an intervention. As I listened to the family describe this man who was the chemical abuser, I began to worry that I might experience my first violent intervention. This particular group had an annoying habit of showing up 15 to 20 minutes late for our meetings. As a rule I always ask the group to be at my office ten minutes before the start of the intervention, but for this group I asked for twenty-five minutes.

On the day of this family's intervention, I had the office chairs set up in a circle and I waited. Thirty-five minutes past the time we were scheduled to begin the intervention, no one had shown up. The individual we were intervening with was driving down alone. I became concerned that he might show up ahead of the rest of the group.

When I heard the elevator bell outside my office ring, I felt a great sense of relief. However, my relief was short-lived. It was the gentleman we were to meet with, not the family. He looked into my office and asked if all this was for him. Not being sure what to do, I introduced myself and said something very profound. I said "Yup."

He then asked if his family was going to talk to him about his drinking.

To which I replied, "Yup."

He wanted to know if in my opinion based as it was on their side of the story, did I think he had a problem with alcohol.

To which I replied, "Yup."

"Are they going to ask me to check into the hospital today?"

"Yup."

"Do you think I should?"

"Yup."

"O.K."

And with that he and I started down the hall to admit him to the hospital. As we passed the elevator and entered the treatment center, his family arrived. They were all set to go. I told them that he had already agreed to treatment but if they wanted, I would see them in my office after he was admitted. They were upset that I didn't make him sit and listen to their prepared statements. But our goal was to get the suffering alcoholic into treatment and we had succeeded.

I also pointed out that all of their preparations were not wasted. Their concern obviously had started him on the process of change even before the actual intervention. The no-talk rule had been broken. And they would have the opportunity to participate in family counseling at the treatment center at which time they would be able to present their feelings and concerns.

More About Your Group Goal

It is not uncommon for the chemically dependent person to want to negotiate a better deal with you. Following the intervention the person may state that with all this new information he or she can take care of the situation without further help. Also, if the person seems willing to accept some type of help, the group may want to back down from the original goal. Or if you have offered several different treatment options that are very different, the chances are excellent that the person will use this confusion to further the belief that he or she doesn't need help. Or the person will choose the least involved form of help.

As a group it is far better to offer a limited number of options. The easiest choice is the one that will be made every time. If you really want the person to enter a hospital but also offer him or her the option of going through an outpatient program or just attending A.A. meetings, it is highly unlikely the person will even consider entering a hospital.

It makes far more sense to offer treatment alternatives that are similar to what the group goal is. For example, if you are asking for inpatient treatment, name two or three local area inpatient centers and possibly one center outside of the local area that are available.

Consistency within the group will make accepting treatment a great deal more likely. Occasionally one member of the group may not feel as strongly about what the goal should be. When this happens, the person might hurt your intervention. As a group you may wish to ask him or her not to participate. This may cause hard feelings for a while, but the long term good that will come from treatment will far outweigh any resentments.

At times one member of the group may think that he or she can talk the person into treatment without help from the group. While this effort will seldom succeed, I generally suggest that if they feel a need to talk with the individual one-on-one, they should. If they are successful in motivating the person you are concerned about into treatment, your goal has been reached. Even if they cannot get the person into treatment, the long standing no talk rule has once again been broken. I view this as one more support being added to the bridge from suffering to surrender.

Sometimes a member of the group will need to do this for his or her own peace of mind. If that's what must happen and if it frees them to participate in the intervention, so much the better.

From time to time a person may threaten to tell the individual everything that is taking place. This form of emotional blackmail sounds far worse than it really is. This is an attempt by a member of the group to control or manipulate the circumstances surrounding the intervention. This will just complicate matters. If they insist on structuring the intervention in ways that are deceptive or manipulative (telling the person you are going out for breakfast when you're actually planning to meet for the intervention), it may be best to remove this person from the group. Recovery from addiction is based on a program of honesty. We can't begin this program of honesty with a lie. If we attempt to deceive or manipulate, we find that since the disease of addiction is the master of manipulation, we will lose.

As a group carefully plan each step of your intervention. Fully prepare and rehearse your written materials as if the person you are worried about is present. Set your goals. Work closely with your chosen treatment center to ensure a smooth entry into treatment. Be honest and direct about what you see and what you want. *Remember the three keys to a successful intervention are common sense, honesty, and compassion.*

8

What To Do When the Intervention is Over

Interventions tend to go very quickly. I have never been involved in an intervention that lasted more than 90 minutes. Usually they are much shorter than that.

Based on my past experience I can say that the most likely outcome of your intervention will be that after some discussion, the individual will agree to enter treatment.

The key to the successful conclusion for an intervention is when the individual acknowledges that he or she will accept help (*not* that he or she is chemically dependent). It would be easy if they just stood up and said, "O.K., let's go," but this is seldom the case. The subject of the intervention is usually much more indirect.

Vernon Johnson, D.D., the originator of the intervention concept, describes this indirect type of acceptance as "alcoholese". The individual makes a statement within a statement. They accept help but in a way that can be very deceiving. The following incident illustrates this point.

A family had come to me to intervene with a woman who was in her mid-to-late forties, and was socially prominent. She was physically very tiny, not much over ninety pounds, but her family was quite afraid of her anger. Her husband, mother and two grown daughters participated in the intervention.

Each member of the group presented his or her list of experiences very well. I acted as a spokesperson that day and summed up the family's wish that she check into the hospital immediately, at which point she exploded. She slammed her fist down on my desk and said, "There is no way I'll check into this hospital today!"

The family was devastated. All of their worst fears were coming true. Some of them began to cry. I asked her what time tomorrow she would check in. She replied that she would be there at nine a.m. (she actually arrived at five after nine).

The "alcoholese" here is that she hadn't said no to treatment, but that's what her family heard. She simply said "not today". She was a socially prominent person in her town and she was scheduled to attend a major fund-raising ball that night. Her family had forgotten to mention during our preparations that she had been active in the planning for the party. In her mind to maintain her public reputation it was necessary that she attend the social event. Even though it was risky to wait an additional day, in this case we chose to.

Since the intervention is based on the value system of the person you are concerned about, these issues should be considered during the planning phase. We realized that waiting was not ideal and had I known of the party I would have planned the intervention for the following day. In this situation the woman was also known to follow through on any promise she made. The family was certain that when she agreed to treatment she would follow through.

In another incident, after an intervention with a man, his sister asked if he wanted to go into treatment. His reply was "No." She pointed out all the reasons why he should want to go, but he still stated that he didn't want to go. At this point I stepped in and asked if he *would* go. He replied that he would, but he did not *want* to go. That may sound like semantics and may even seem a little silly, but to him it was a very important point.

Once the individual agrees to go to treatment, the spokesperson should take him or her to the center immediately. Bags can always be packed by family members and brought over later. It is important to follow through on the agreement as quickly as possible.

Members of the group can hug the person and thank him or her for agreeing to go to treatment. But there should be no lengthy conversation. Standing around talking can lead to a very subtle swing in the mood of the group and the individual. When this occurs, the individual may take advantage of the chance to have a change of heart.

What To Do If Things Go Wrong

Of course not every intervention proceeds perfectly smoothly. Some individuals might leave the room. This is not always the end of the intervention. Sometimes they really need to stand or leave the room for a few minutes. Whenever possible we try to discourage such interruptions, but they may happen.

If the person leaves the room, do not physically stop him or her. Let a few minutes pass and as a group decide who may be able to convince him or her to come back in. The person selected should go to the individual and point out that the group cares, is concerned and would really appreciate his or her returning. Indicate that the group realizes it's not easy, but it is important.

If they refuse to come back into the room, you still have options. In one case where this occurred, the family followed the person from my office to the parking lot and continued the intervention there with success. I later found out that the individual had left because he felt embarrassed to have a stranger hear what he considered to be terrible things about him.

The solidarity of the group can have a major influence on whether or not treatment is accepted immediately. I urge all group members to make a commitment to each other that they will stand together. Sometimes this can seem harsh and unreasonable, especially if the group has decided to cut off financial or other forms of support if treatment is refused. In the long run however, this can be the most effective means to allow a chemically dependent person to feel directly the consequences of the chemical use.

Not all groups will make a strong commitment to the goal. Don't lose hope. While this may slow down the desired outcome, it doesn't mean your intervention won't work.

In one intervention it seemed as if nothing would ever go right. One of the participants took the individual out drinking to tell him about the group's concern and the details of the intervention. Other family members wouldn't stop fighting long enough to decide if they would help. And the wife was unable to set a bottom line if the dependent person refused to seek help.

With all this against us, we went ahead as best we could and got to the point where we asked him to enter the hospital. He informed us that he had already quit and he didn't need help. He was unwilling to budge from this stance. With no bottom line from the family, no leverage that they were willing to use, the intervention came to an end without his entering treatment.

Some weeks later I saw him in one of the rooms at the hospital. I stopped in and asked him what had happened. He said he could not turn off what had been said the day of the intervention. Each time he went drinking after that day, he heard the intervention over again. He smiled and said that he knew the day of the intervention his drinking was over. The only question left was how much more he could get away with. He then said that when he got home, his wife had changed. She hadn't threatened him or thrown him out, she no longer enabled him. He couldn't get away with it any more.

This was an exceptional situation. We were lucky that he entered treatment. It is vital for the group to follow through on the group goals, even if the individual doesn't go into treatment immediately. By establishing beforehand the actions you will take if the person does not choose to accept help, you increase the likelihood of success in the long run. Some people call this the "what if" clause (like "what if I don't go to treatment?"). Others call it the "hammer clause". Basically it means that as a group and as individuals you have decided that you will no longer enable the person. If at the conclusion of the intervention there is no way the individual is willing to enter treatment, spell out without threats or judgments what you are going to do differently.

All too often the natural reaction of some group members is to make threats. Statements about divorce, the loss of a job or the withdrawal of all financial aid may sound frightening, but unless you *fully* intend to carry through with such action, don't make the statement. Threatening the loss of a job means nothing if an employer is not willing to fire the employee.

The prospect of losing a job can be an excellent motivator if used properly. If as an employer you are at the point of firing the employee, let him or her know it. But phrase it so as not to set up a confrontation of egos. You can say that the job will be waiting for him or her after treatment, but you really can't afford to keep the person unless he or she goes to treatment. This places the responsibility for deciding on the individual. Their actions, not yours, determine whether or not they keep their job. Remember that we are dealing with a person who is not thinking clearly. We don't need to crush them. We can allow them to save face if they will accept treatment immediately.

If you are a family member, you are taking an emotional risk. As a person who cares you probably have been caught in the trap of enabling. It's impossible to have been involved closely and not suffered with the addict. Because of this you will need to take care of yourself as well. For your well-being and that of the addict, participate in the treatment center's family program.

If you find yourself saying, "Geez, I'd like to go, but I don't have the time," then you know how the addict feels. For each reason you have to avoid participating fully, figure out a reason why you must. If you are unwilling to make the necessary arrangements to participate, you will deprive yourself of one of the most moving and beneficial experiences of your life. Besides it's inconsistent to ask the addict to get help under any circumstances and then be unwilling yourself.

Whether or not the person you are intervening with enters treatment immediately, you should get help for yourself. As a family you can become active in Alateen or Al-Anon, programs intended for the families of chemically dependent people. Local treatment centers and family therapists have special programs for the recovery of the family members. Take advantage of these programs.

The disease of addiction causes people to withdraw and become lonely. This loneliness can affect everyone. Family members do have the right to recover with or without the addicted person. They can overcome their own loneliness. In fact, by the family's commitment to recovery, the addicted person may join them in treatment when they can see the family is serious.

In one intervention we had an extremely intelligent person we were hoping to reach. The group consisted of his wife and two children. The intervention did not go well from the beginning. He was unwilling even to enter my office and stayed in the waiting room. As a family they sat and discussed some of the options available to them. The medical director of the center even spent some time with him, but after an hour the man left.

Although he was unwilling to accept help, the family decided that it could no longer continue as it had. The new plan for the family was to see a local family therapist, who suggested that they attend Al-Anon, which they did for several months.

Some time later I was walking down the hall of the treatment center and glanced into a group room. The man was sitting in a chair waiting for group counseling to start. He gave me a dirty look and somewhat sarcastically informed me that "Your blank . . . blank . . . intervention didn't work on me." The goal of the intervention is to help those who suffer from addiction. The claim that intervention hadn't worked sounded ironic since he was in treatment. It did not occur as quickly as we would have liked, and it certainly wasn't a textbook intervention, but the goal was met.

If someone you love or care about suffers from addiction, so do you. *Get Help.* With intervention the entire family can begin to recover together. Even if the individual doesn't enter treatment immediately, the family can proceed with its recovery. And as often as not when family members do, the chemically dependent person will follow.

I am a strong advocate of Al-Anon. When you read the first step in their program of recovery you see that it says, "We admitted we were powerless over alcohol — that our lives had become unmanageable."

If you examine your list of examples prepared for the intervention, you will see that you are, in fact, powerless over the chemical use. All you need to do is remember the times you tried to control it. As you look at the adjustments you may have made, no matter how subtle or small that they may have seemed, you can point to the times your life was unmanageable.

9

What To Expect In Treatment

Many treatment centers work with families prior to admission with a pre-admission service. This is an opportunity to verify insurance coverage, meet with the staff and ask questions that each of you have. Again I encourage people to familiarize themselves with the appropriate facilities before the intervention.

When the person you have intervened with enters treatment, the first person they are probably going to meet will be the intake counselor who will gather some basic information: the patient's full name, age, social security number, etc. At this point the admission process is no different from that in any other part of a hospital.

The second person to meet with the new patient is usually a nurse. However, if the individual is in bad physical condition where there may be concern for withdrawal problems, a doctor is brought in immediately. The nurse will evaluate the patient by checking blood pressure and pulse. There will also be a series of questions asked about the patient's past medical history. This information is then passed on to the doctor, who will do a physical examination and decide which, if any, medicines are required for detoxification. From time to time a patient may not require any medicine. If this is the case, so much the better. That usually means the patient can begin the program immediately.

If medication is required, it will be used to ensure a safe withdrawal. The potential for medical problems during withdrawal requires that all possible precautions be followed.

The Inpatient Program

Up to this point the admission procedure is fairly standard, no matter which center is selected. But each treatment center has its own way of describing the different aspects of treatment once the patient is admitted. For an inpatient program there are generally five basic steps.

Step one: Primary care. This is the phase of treatment where the patient is medically evaluated, withdrawn from whichever drug(s) they are on and introduced to the treatment center's daily routine.

Often during this part of the program the patient begins to participate in group activities with other chemically dependent people. One of the most important activities will be the writing of an autobiography and history of the patient's drug and alcohol use.

The goal here is to assist the patient to break through the denial by examining the personal impact that chemicals have had.

Step two: Recovery. The second phase of the program is reached when the patient has completed both detoxification and step one. In the recovery phase the patient begins to participate in all treatment activities. Since this disease is so devastating in so many areas of an individual's life, the patient can only be *exposed* to all the elements of recovery; and he or she must continue to participate in the activities once treatment is ended.

Included in this part of the program will be group counseling, individual counseling, education sessions, physical fitness and very importantly, attendance at self-help meetings (Alcoholics Anonymous, Narcotics Anonymous, etc.).

During this process patients will begin to identify with other patients and their stories and they will begin the final stages of acceptance of the disease. While in recovery, they will use all of the defenses that have worked up to now to avoid facing the need to change. The weight of group and individual counseling and the educational sessions help to take down the shield. Additionally through the course of treatment the patient is exposed to other recovering people with various lengths of sobriety. This exposure will help the patient learn that recovery is a positive experience.

Step three: Family care program. I set this out as a separate component because family members have a responsibility to participate in the recovery process. This serves two purposes.

1. While the patient is responsible for his or her own recovery, the family will play an important role. If the individual goes through treatment without family care, the "no-talk rules" will still exist. Trying to recover when everyone is walking around on egg shells creates a tremendous pressure for everyone in the house.
2. Since the family members are also very much affected by this disease, you deserve treatment for your own peace of mind. Regardless of whether or not the chemically dependent person follows through with his or her own recovery, family members can. Participation in a family care program can free you from the nagging feelings of guilt, shame and inadequacy.

Some facilities offer very structured programs for family care. These models are designed to begin a series of family communication experiences. No family program can hope to provide all that is needed but like the chemical dependency treatment goals, it will ensure exposure to the essentials.

Most family programs include group counseling (with and without the chemically dependent person), educational sessions and attendance at self-help meetings. These meetings include Al-Anon, Alateen, Adult Children of Alcoholics (ACoA) and others. In some instances, ongoing supportive family therapy with a specially trained professional may be recommended following treatment.

Step four: Re-entry. This is the time set aside to help the patient begin to plan for his or her discharge from the treatment facility.

During this phase of treatment patients begin to identify which A.A. meetings they will attend after leaving the center. And patients are encouraged to select an A.A. member who will become their sponsor. Sponsoring is an informal relationship where a long-time member of A.A. helps the newer member with the early questions of sobriety.

During this time planning for aftercare will occur. This frequently involves the significant people in the chemically dependent person's life. From my experience I believe that wherever possible, the employer, spouse and anyone else involved should be a part of the planning. The plan should include which aftercare group(s) will be attended, identification of those actions that constitute warning signs for a possible relapse and what actions the group will take to lessen the likelihood of a relapse.

Step five: Aftercare program. This is usually a peer group of former patients with varying lengths of sobriety. They share with each other some of the problems they have faced since they left treatment and discuss what they did to overcome these problems.

Aftercare programs should include the family as well as the patient. Even if the patient experiences a temporary relapse, the family should continue in its own recovery. The family does this for its own well-being. If the family stops the enabling cycle, the chemically dependent person usually gets back into recovery.

Aftercare programs vary in length from three months to two years. Most follow-up studies suggest that the longer an individual stays active in a treatment environment, the greater his or her chance for recovery.

Aftercare, relapse prevention planning and self-help groups provide a safety net for the newly recovered person.

Outpatient Services

Outpatient programs are frequently scaled-down versions of inpatient programs. They include the fundamental aspects of treatment similar to the inpatient program. The most noticeable differences come in the area of detoxification and re-entry planning.

People in need of considerable medical management for detoxification are usually poor candidates for outpatient programs. Re-entry planning for the outpatient is also different since the individual has been living a fairly normal life while in treatment.

Treatment Results

Regardless of the type of treatment program and the talent of the staff, no center can guarantee results. However, even if the patient does not respond immediately, that doesn't mean that treatment has failed.

As long as the family has begun to recover, it is difficult for the addicted person to continue in the disease. A friend of mine likes to say that a belly full of scotch just isn't as much fun once you've had a head full of A.A. or when your family stops enabling. No treatment program and no family member can force sobriety on anyone. But they can make recovery desirable.

Keep in mind, however, many successfully recovering people began a rather reluctant involvement when forced into a program by a judge or employer. The point is recovery can begin only after some kind of exposure to recovery. And in a treatment center the likelihood of recovery increases because the individual is constantly exposed to sobriety.

The final decision to recover rests with the chemically dependent person. Is he or she willing and able to do what is required to recover? As family and friends we can encourage and support recovery. However, we must accept the fact that we cannot control the outcome.

What Can Be Expected of the Patient?

It is reasonable to assume that since the patient has taken many years to get to the point where they are now, they will not be changed overnight. The series of defenses that have been developed are well entrenched. To break through these will take time and patience. Even as improvement is seen, there will be days when it seems as if nothing has changed at all. Don't be discouraged by this. When you look back after several months you'll be amazed by all that has changed.

As an individual enters treatment he or she will resent being there. Since no one wants to be sick, this is normal. Often family members will want the patient to be grateful for helping them into treatment. My experience shows that this will come — but with time, not during the first week or two.

Since denial is normal, the patient entering treatment will most probably deny the need to be there. He or she will minimize the seriousness of the problem. As the patient begins group activities, he or she will show a variety of defenses. Again this is normal. Acting angry, trying to charm staff and other patients, withdrawing and being aloof are attempts to keep the no-talk rule in place.

At some point the patient may seem to be depressed. These reactions should be seen for what they are: natural progression. Most professionals in the field of chemical dependency will tell you that if a patient walks into treatment saying all the right words and walks out the same way without going through the whole range of feelings, he or she doesn't stand much of a chance to stay sober.

If the patient seems angry, believe it or not, that is a fairly good sign. The staff has a feeling level to start with. If the patient has gone from admission to immediate acceptance, then there's cause to worry.

Remember, with any disease before there is acceptance there will be denial, anger, bargaining and depression. Don't let these reactions scare you. Without them, full recovery isn't likely.

What Can Be Expected of Family Members?

As a participant in the disease process of chemical dependency, you develop a specific defensive lifestyle to counteract that of the addicted person. Since this represents a major disease process, it is reasonable to expect that you will go through the same type of recovery process as the individual who has been admitted for the addiction.

It's normal for family members to try to deny that they have suffered because of the disease. Yet if you have altered your lifestyle at all (covered up for the person, missed social engagements or tried to control the chemical use at all), you've been affected.

Some family members react angrily when you suggest that they participate in family treatment. They often say something like, "I'm not the one who drank. It's her problem." If you insist that they cooperate, you will probably hear the bargaining begin. "I'll go to one meeting. But I just can't go to all of them."

The depression is there as well. It is difficult to surrender their very effective defenses. There has been a payoff for these defenses, whether it was acting as a martyr, appearing to be the strong one or being known as the one who holds the family together. Once recovery begins, the relationship patterns within the family must change and each member loses whatever payoff they were getting from their enabling behavior. When the sharing of family responsibilities begins, we see acceptance and true family recovery.

10

Life After Treatment

Leaving the treatment center may seem as frightening as entering it did. There is certainly no guarantee about what will happen next.

From my experience the best indicator for success is sticking with the program of recovery learned in treatment. Each member of the family takes responsibility for his or her own recovery and follows through on the recommendations for aftercare and self-help groups regardless of what other family members do. After a while most of the fears will evaporate.

Most concerns seem to center around what can we do to have fun now that he or she is not drinking. Of course, the simple answer is "anything you darn well want to do". One of the freedoms of recovery is not having to worry about whether the addicted person will drink or use drugs. The reality is that we live in a world filled with alcohol and other drugs. There is no way humanly possible to shelter the addict or alcoholic from this fact. Nor do we need to. We also live in a world filled with sugar. People that suffer from diabetes do not expect that those around them to stop eating sugar just because they have.

It would be equally unrealistic for the chemically dependent person or a family member to expect others to alter their lives to accommodate the addict or alcoholic. It sounds trite to say, but true friends seldom are offended by sobriety. They may not understand alcoholism or the need for abstinence but they will not make an issue of it.

Traveling will be a great deal more fun for everyone. Whether it's to an A.A. convention or that long dreamed of tour of Europe. There is a freedom to go anywhere and do anything. The only difference is that the recovering person is far less likely to do anything that will cause themselves or others embarrassment or harm.

When there are invitations to parties where the sole purpose is getting loaded, the recovering person may try going to a few but soon will drop them simply because they're not much fun. At parties where people may be drinking as a component of the party, not the main reason for the get-together, there should be no problem in attending.

Occasionally someone may comment on the recovering person not joining in. Or someone may assure the recovering person that one drink can't hurt. No doubt the recovering person will inform this person of the decision not to drink but if they persist in their offer of alcohol or drugs, you have the option of leaving. Another freedom of sobriety seems to be the recognition that we no longer need to prove anything by sitting through unnecessary or uncomfortable situations like this.

The most important thing to remember is that recovery means returning to a normal life. A part of the condition known as being human means we will have times in life that are wonderful and some that are painful, times that are exciting and others that are boring, challenging or mundane.

The recovering chemically dependent person as well as the family members learn to roll with the punches. Together the family can grow and do anything as a family that they choose to.

By the very nature of this disease we know that relapse is always a possibility. With this in mind it clearly shows the value of living one day at a time. A relapse may occur in a family member, not just the drinker. By sticking with your recovery program you'll find the peace of mind that you are looking for. Should a relapse occur, view it as a temporary setback. Your life will continue. Take care of your needs, remember not to enable and the chances for a full recovery are excellent.

11

Why We Keep Trying

More than ever I believe that we keep trying simply because it's the right thing to do. Whether we are family or friend, health care provider or educator, we have a responsibility to, not for, recovery.

There is one other excellent reason for using an intervention to achieve your goal. A clinical study from the Rimrock Foundation of Billings, Montana, evaluated the likelihood of recovery when a patient has entered treatment through intervention. According to David Cunningham, the administrator for the Rimrock Foundation program, a patient that enters treatment without an intervention should be intervened upon within the first four days of treatment. The impact of the intervention will significantly reduce the number of patients leaving without completing care and will increase their chances for recovery.

Knowing as we do that the chemically dependent person cannot see the extent of his or her illness, an outside influence must be used. But I have been called a meddler and asked how I can justify what seems to be such an intrusion in a person's life.

I developed my answer to these questions by stepping back to look at the broad picture. I'm aware that in the final analysis the chemically dependent people must make their own decisions. I also know that for them to make the decisions, it's critical to show them what their options are. Honesty mixed with common sense and compassion do not equal intruding. When someone's chemical use affects our lives, we have a right to voice our concern.

I once read a book that seemed to define the emotional state of the chemically dependent person better that any I had ever seen. This book was not written about addiction, however. The title of this book is *"Man's Search For Meaning"* by Dr. Viktor Frankl. It is based on his experiences in a Nazi concentration camp.

In his book Dr. Frankl talks about the prisoner as a person stripped of the future. The sentence in the camps was unlimited. The phrase used to describe this was "a provisional existence of unknown limit". With no end to the sentence and only the uncertainty, the future as we know it ceased to exist.

Dr. Frankl went on to say, "It is a peculiarity of man that he can only live by looking to the future." Without this basic need being met, normal life is over.

The internal pain of addiction means being trapped in the past. The addicted person experiences a decaying of the spirit and of the person. The continual abuse of chemicals followed by the emotional pain creates a void. The outside world can be seen but not touched. Even the experiences of time changes dramatically. A day for the addicted person can seem to last forever while weeks pass very quickly.

The continued inner conflicts bring the chemically dependent person to his or her own provisional existence of unknown limit. The active use of chemicals provides temporary relief, but that is followed by a retreat into the past. Attempting to regain a time when it was fun, we see this individual being trapped.

Cynicism permeates the spirit. As the progression of the disease goes unchecked we see the chemically dependent person blocked from all that is important. They are robbed of the very essence of life. That which is needed most to survive is gone. The disease prevents them from having a future. With no real hope for the future there's no true quality of life left. Only a repetition of the painful present.

Seen through the eyes of a drug-affected brain life no longer holds the hope or promise of the future that we need. The small joys will be clung to unreasonably while the letdowns can appear devastating. The suffering is unbearable.

In Alcoholics Anonymous the basic tenet is that when the suffering becomes unbearable, the alcoholic will "hit bottom". When the excuses no longer work and the pain is too great, the person is ready to go to any length to recover.

In the A.A. literature they describe a need to develop a belief in a Higher Power (an individual chooses any concept that will work for him or her; some say God, while others use different concepts).

In many A.A. stories I've heard the suffering alcoholic state that they begged God to help them. But however desperate or sincere the pleading individual may be, the cries for help go unanswered. Since there is no plan for action and no true understanding of the problem by the addicted person, change won't occur.

Spinoza said, "Emotion, which is suffering, ceases to be suffering as soon as we form a clear and precise picture of it." From within this framework, the chemically dependent person begging God for relief must continue to suffer, since no clear and precise picture of the suffering is available to the drug impaired mind.

As family or friend can we allow this suffering to go unchecked? Intervention provides the clear and precise picture the chemically dependent person needs to move from suffering.

A major reason for undertaking this effort is you. You actually win when you break the no-talk rule. As you begin to recover from the co-dependency, you build on your future. As you break the cycle of enabling, you will also make it possible for the individual you are concerned about to enter the future as well.

I've chosen my profession to be in human service. Working with families, industry and other health care professionals in relieving the misery of addiction is very rewarding for me. It is my hope that by following the suggestions in this book you too will experience one of the greatest joys a person can: the opportunity to help save a life. The only requirement for effective action is a caring attitude and a belief that *Alcoholism doesn't have to win.*

Checklist For Intervention

Prior to your intervention make sure you cover all the bases.

_____ **Draft a list of potential interveners**

- Remember to let them be responsible for saying yes or no.

_____ **Contact each person on your list**

- Face to face wherever possible.

Write Out List of Examples

_____ **Identify the changes in their pattern of chemical use**

- Amount consumed.
- Denial of use, even when it's obvious.
- Hiding the frequency or amount being used.
- Attempts to control or go on the wagon.

_____ **Identify changes in personality**

- Angry outbursts followed by acting as if nothing occurred.
- Violent outbursts.
- Silly or irrational actions.
- Obsessed with drinking or drug related activities.
- How does this contrast with their sober behavior.

_____ **Identify health problems**

* Broken bones and bruises, possibly unexplained.
* Frequent stomach problems.
* Blackouts (chemically induced amnesia).
* Depression.
* Use of multiple doctors/pharmacies for prescribed drugs.

_____ **Identify legal problems**

* Arrested for driving under the influence (or describe the times when arrests were possible).
* Financial problems (i.e., higher insurance rates, etc.).
* Stealing of valuables (teenagers seldom earn enough money to support the disease of addiction).

_____ **Identify disruptions in personal activities**

* Dropping hobbies or activities that interfere with chemical use.
* Loss of jobs or promotions.
* Significant drop in grades at school.
* A shift in usual circle of friends (usually towards others that use chemicals in the same manner).

_____ **Identify problems that have occurred during special occasions**

* Christmas.
* Thanksgiving.
* Birthdays.
* Anniversaries.
* Parties.

Setting Up the Intervention

_____ Investigate treatment center options.
_____ Verify treatment costs and insurance coverage.
_____ Set the group goals.
_____ Select the spokesperson for the group.
_____ Choose the order of presentation.

_____ Write a letter of concern that covers
- * How you feel towards the person.
- * Address any feelings of fear you have.
- * Talk about how long you've been worried.

Remember that this letter will lead into your list of concerns.
_____ Fully rehearse all lists.
_____ Develop suitable answers to why "I can't go right now."
_____ Select the time and the location for the intervention.

Resources

With your willingness to intervene you will discover several features that you may not have counted on. One of the most important of these is that you are no longer alone.

If after reading this book, you feel you want to find a professional intervention counselor you can check with your local treatment center. If they don't have a specially trained intervention counselor (give them your copy of this book), call The Intervention Referral Network at (619) 693-1433 in San Diego, California.

While I was on the staff at Scripps Memorial Hospital Alcoholism Treatment Center I began collecting the names of intervention counselors around the country. Today on this Intervention Referral Network we have over 145 intervention programs listed in thirty-four states. Some of them will travel. These are excellent potential resources. Wherever possible I suggest you prepare for your intervention with the help and guidance of an intervention counselor. We keep this list so you can call for a referral.

Other excellent sources of information are no further away than your telephone book. Usually located under Alcoholism in the yellow pages (sometimes under Drug Services). These sources include:

* National Council on Alcoholism
  Headquarters in New York City with offices throughout the country.

* Employee Assistance Programs offered through the individual's company
* Military Treatment Centers worldwide for active duty personnel
* Veterans Administration Hospitals for former service personnel
* Al-Anon, Al-Anon Adult Children of Alcoholics and Alateen Family Groups
  POB 862 Midtown Station
  New York, NY 10018-086
* Alcoholics Anonymous
  Box 459 Grand Central Station
  New York, NY 10163
* Adult Children of Alcoholics
  POB 35623
  Los Angeles, CA 90035
* Batterers Anonymous
  POB 29
  Redlands, CA 92373
* Divorce Anonymous
  POB 5313
  Chicago, IL 60680
* Emotions Anonymous
  POB 4245
  St. Paul, MN 55104
* Families Anonymous
  POB 344
  Torrance, CA 90501
* Families in Action
  Suite 300
  3845 North Druid Hills Road
  Decatur, GA 30033
* Incest Survivors Anonymous
  POB 5613
  Long Beach, CA 90805

* Nar-Anon Family Groups
  350 5th Street, Suite 207
  San Pedro, CA 90731

* Narcotics Anonymous
  POB 9999
  Van Nuys, CA 91409

* National Single Parent Coalition
  10 West 23 Street
  New York, NY 10010

* Overeaters Anonymous
  4025 Spenser Street, Suite 203
  Torrance, CA 90503

* Parents Anonymous
  22330 Hawthorne Boulevard
  Torrance, CA 90505

* Parents Without Partners
  7910 Woodmont Avenue
  Washington, DC 20014

* Pill-Anon Family Programs
  POB 120 Gracie Station
  New York, NY 10028

* Pills Anonymous
  POB 473 Ansonia Station
  New York, NY 10023

* Prison Families Anonymous
  134 Jackson Street
  Hempstead, NY 11550

* Single Dad's Hotline
  POB 4842
  Scottsdale, AZ 85258